Stone Age Diary

STONE AGE DIARY

The Story of John and Janine Schultz

by John and Janine Schultz

Christian Publications

CAMP HILL, PENNSYLVANIA

Christian Publications, Inc.
3825 Hartzdale Drive, Camp Hill, Pennsylvania 17011
www.cpi-horizon.com
www.christianpublications.com

Faithful, biblical publishing since 1883

Stone Age Diary
ISBN: 0-87509-918-1
LOC Catalog Control Number: 00-136393
© 2001 by Christian Publications, Inc.
All rights reserved
Printed in the United States of America

01 02 03 04 05   5 4 3 2 1

Cover illustration by Karl Foster

Unless otherwise indicated,
Scripture taken from the HOLY BIBLE:
NEW INTERNATIONAL VERSION ®.
Copyright © 1973, 1978, 1984 by the
International Bible Society. Used by
permission of Zondervan Bible Publishers.

Dedicated
to our four children:

Ruthy Hall
J.P. Schultz
Mitch Schultz
Viviane Miner
and their lovely families

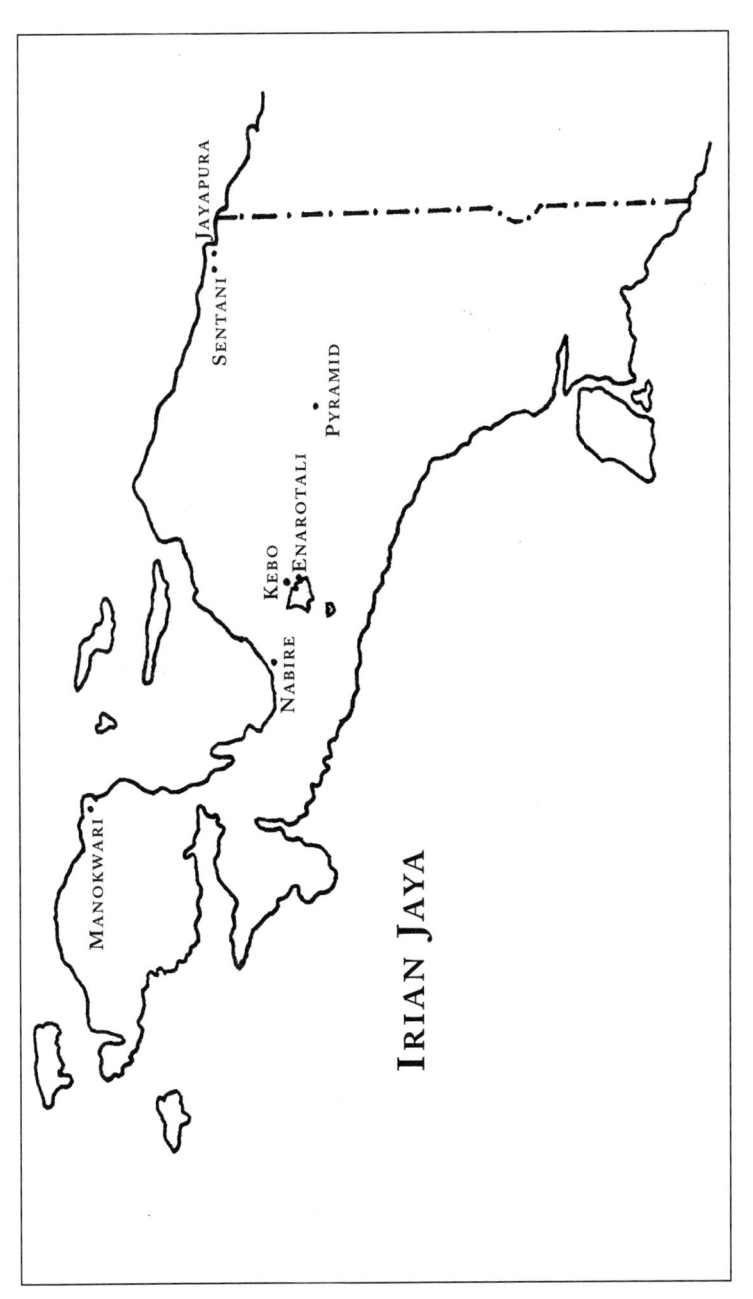

Contents

Foreword xi
Preface xiii
1 The War 1
2 The Call 16
3 Stone Age Shock 35
4 War—and the Jungle Adventure 48
5 The People Who Heal People 63
6 Sometimes the Twain Do Meet 74
7 Rough but Precious Jewels 86
8 The Empire Strikes Back 101
9 A Few Grams of Uranium 115
10 Hond and Some Lessons in Forgiveness 127
11 Rebellion, Revival and Readjustment 136
12 Tears Bigger than Mine 148
13 The Lord's Doing 160
14 A Fiery Fence and DDT 175
15 Turning Points 187
16 "Missionary Stuff" 198
17 Jack of All Trades 209
18 As Close to the End of the World as One Can Get 220
19 . . . Such Sweet Sorrow 230
Appendix: Final Report to the Irian Jaya Field Forum 236

Foreword

John Schultz, a Dutch speaker from Holland, married Janine, a French speaker from Belgium. Could they find happiness as part of a team of English-speaking missionaries teaching in the Ekari language in a remote region of Indonesian-speaking Southeast Asia?

Happiness, yes! And much, much more!

In his youth John trained as a piano tuner. Now, some piano tuners tune pianos but cannot play them. But piano tuner John Schultz, once he has got a piano on key, not only plays it—he even makes it resound with the fugues of Johann Sebastian Bach.

Similarly, many Christians understand the Bible for themselves but are not skilled to teach it. John and Janine, already knowing the Bible in Dutch and French, went on to comprehend and teach it in three other languages as well.

Those they nurtured spiritually over more than three decades as teachers range from cultured Westerners and Indonesians to illiterate Stone Age Ekari people in Irian Jaya.

Few Christians indeed have experienced the range of trials, sorrows and joys that awaited John and Janine among the warring tribes of Indonesia's Irian Jaya province. This, their intriguing *Stone Age Diary,* is herewith open for you. Relive with them their trauma as children in Second-World-War Europe.

Share John's pain as the stabbed victim of a ruthless Indonesian brigand.

Learn from their struggle to parent their own children adequately while shouldering the demands that come with training shepherds for hundreds of young churches.

Have they found happiness? Yes. But theirs is much more than happiness defined merely as personal satisfaction. Theirs is a happiness that can never be complete in this world, but is sure to be both complete and eternal beyond this world. It is the happiness of those who have sought first the kingdom of God and His will, no matter how dear the cost.

Don Richardson
Pasadena, California
November 1998

Preface

As I opened the door of the Alliance dormitory, I bumped into Jonathan. I had just completed a week of exhausting committee meetings, and I was ready for bed. Five-year-old Jonathan looked at me.

"Who are you?" he asked.

"I am John Schultz. And who are you?"

"I am Jonathan. What do you do? Are you a pilot?"

"No."

"Are you a mechanic?" (Obviously, Jonathan was thinking of the Mission Aviation Fellowship and their base in Sentani.)

"No."

"What do you do then?"

"I'm a missionary."

"Oh, you're like my daddy. You do nothing!"

This book is not written in defense of little Jonathan's accusation, but Janine and I want him and you to know that not just pilots and mechanics work on the mission field.

Neither is the purpose of our writing to display how much we accomplished, although some things of lasting value were planted and grew.

What we do want to do is to take you to a place where only a few decades ago people were still living in the Stone Age, and we want to tell you about some of the amazing ways those people reacted to the gospel of Jesus Christ.

A lot of what we did during our thirty-eight years in Irian Jaya was common, mundane, routine. Since retiring from active overseas missionary service and now being able to look back over the years, we marvel at the adventures into which the Lord led us. We experienced His presence in ways we could never have even dreamed.

When we first said, "Here we are, send us," we had no idea what we were in for. But now we can testify that it was a most exciting quest in which He showed

> His grace when we failed,
> His love when we hurt,
> His glory when we sank in the mud.

We have written this book primarily to say "thank you" to the Lord, but also to say "thank you" to those of you who made it possible for us to go and who upheld us while we were there.

1

The War

The day dawned in all of its spring glory that May 10, 1940 at our family home in the Netherlands. But things would never be the same. It was to be the beginning of a long, dark winter in the world's history.

I awoke to the droning sound of airplanes overhead and jumped out of bed with excitement. Holland was at war. When I heard the news, my ten-year-old patriotic heart told me that the Dutch army would "lick the Nazis in no time." Little could I anticipate the years of cruel oppression, sadistic terror, senseless persecution and gnawing hunger that lay ahead of us. A long winter of five years under Nazi rule would have been impossible for me to imagine. In fact, it would take years before I would even be able to sort out the emotions that would scar my young life.

It didn't take the Nazis long to tighten their fist and organize their criminal schemes. Within weeks, all Dutch citizens had to register and were issued an ID card. For the Jewish section of the population, the word "Jew" was stamped on the card, and a yellow Star of David was given to them to wear on their coats. Public parks posted signs saying, "Jews Not Allowed." Department stores announced that they would no longer serve Jewish customers.

The Nazis' real intent became clear when, one night early in February 1941, the whole population of the Jewish ghetto of Amsterdam, the capital city of the Netherlands, was taken into custody and transported to German concentration camps. The general public reacted spontaneously by unanimously going on strike. But the evil authorities had anticipated this kind of reaction and had taken a group of prominent citizens into detention as hostages. A large group of them were lined up in a public place and executed before the eyes of the horrified population. Within a few hours, the backbone of the strike had been broken. From that time, all resistance was carried out underground.

Other Jews, trying to escape the fate of those who had been carried off, went into hiding. Several Dutch citizens opened their homes to the secret guests. As the war continued, food shortage became more and more severe, and one needed food rationing coupons to be able to buy staple items in the stores. My father was an employee of the municipal food rationing office in downtown Haarlem, one of the oldest cities on the west shore of the Netherlands. He was in charge of the booklets of coupons that were given out. In this capacity he came into contact with the ten Boom family[1] and made periodic visits to their residence to deliver a supply of food rationing booklets.

On February 29, 1944, my father rang the doorbell at the house of the ten Boom home. A policeman opened the door, pointed a gun at him and told him to come inside. He had been standing outside with his hands in his pockets, fingering a few food stamps, but knowing that the bulk of his delivery was safely hidden in his undershirt. Suddenly nothing was safe anymore. If the stamps were discovered, he would not only go to prison, but he would also endanger the whole clandestine operation. It had obviously been betrayed, and the house had been raided the night before. My father was caught in the net the police had set up for subsequent visitors to the house.

His immediate reaction to this unexpected crisis was to clutch the loose food stamps in his hand and bring his hand to his mouth in his effort to stop a sudden cough. This brought the food stamps safely into his mouth. Pretending that he was too startled to speak in the face of the gun that was pointed on his chest did not take much talent, and soon the stamps were softened enough so that he could swallow them. The police officer did not bother to search him on the spot, nor did the ones who were on guard at the police headquarters where he was taken and where the whole ten Boom family had spent a sleepless night. After a while, my dad was allowed to use the toilet, where he flushed down the incriminating evidence. Nobody ever left a toilet so relieved as was my father! He was then shipped off to the prison for political prisoners in Scheveningen, in the western part of Holland, where he spent six weeks in a cell meant for one person but occupied by four.

One neighbor on our street was a German who had migrated to the Netherlands between the two world wars. Having been born in Germany, he had served in the military during World War I, and it so happened that he was in the same regiment with a certain corporal by the name of Adolph Hitler. When Hitler came to power, his old buddies were all issued a badge indicating that they were personal acquaintances of the Fuehrer.

Herr Kappelmeier was not a Nazi. When he heard that Mr. Schultz had been arrested, being convinced of his innocence, on which point we did not enlighten him, he went to the headquarters of the German police. For any other Dutchman this place would have been off limits, but when Herr Kappelmeier showed his badge, the doors were opened wide for him. He asked the police to open a file on my father. It still took the Nazi bureaucracy six weeks before my dad was called out of his cell, and a Nazi officer questioned him.

"What were you doing at the ten Boom's residence?" he asked.

My father did not want to tell a lie, but he also did not want to tell the truth, since that would endanger the lives of many.

"I have this watch that doesn't work," he answered as he produced the antique gold watch that used to belong to my grandfather. I don't know why he ever bothered to carry it with him because, for as long as I can remember, the watch never worked. But it certainly came in handy at that moment.

"The ten Booms have a watchmaker shop," he added.

He did not say that he had come to have his watch repaired. He made two separate statements, and left it up to the Nazi officer to fuse the two. I don't know whether the man saw through my father's pretext, and it could be that he was under order to let my dad go. Anyhow, after signing a paper, my father was released. Since food had not been plentiful in prison, he came home starved—but free.

We thought that after this harrowing experience our father would withdraw from the danger zone, but the opposite turned out to be true. From that time on, we also began to harbor Jews in our home. They would usually come for a short time and leave after one or two nights. However, on one occasion a Jewish lady with her sixteen-year-old son, about my age, stayed for several weeks.

It was a particularly difficult period of the war. The invasion had taken place in Normandy, and the Allied troops had liberated France and Belgium. They tried to capture the Dutch city of Arnhem, but they lost that battle.[2] This setback made them change their strategy. Instead of liberating the western part of Holland, where we lived, the army moved into Germany, cutting off the German troops in Holland from their homeland. So the German occupational forces no longer received any supplies, and they began to requisition all the food that was meant for the Dutch population. The Dutch began to starve, and in the three western provinces 185,000 people died of starvation between September 1944 and May 1945. The only items available on the food rationing stamps were half a loaf of bread per person per week and one pound of potatoes per person per week. People began to "invent" food, such as stewed tulip bulbs. To make matters worse, we had "guests" who did not bring any food stamps.

One day, in early December, the Germans, being bored with inactivity, decided to comb the whole city of Haarlem for what they called "undesirable elements." And we were harboring Jews! The soldiers came and searched all the houses on the opposite side of our street. Then, instead of crossing over to our side, they went around the block. When my father saw that for a while there were no German soldiers in sight, he sent me across the street to neighbors who were members of the same Christian Reformed Church we belonged to. I asked them if they were willing to hide our guests. I can still picture the lady of the house, an old shriveled-up woman.

When I asked her if she would open her home for Jews, she knew what the consequences would be if she were caught. Yet, without hesitation, she said, "Sure, bring them over."

I was not a Christian at that time. Later, after I had accepted the Lord, I often criticized the members of the Christian Reformed Church for their lack of a positive confession. They would never say that they were born again or that they had accepted the Lord. Their favorite statement was: "We adhere to our principles." Looking back upon this incident, I have modified my criticism considerably. If "adhering to one's principles" means being willing to risk one's life at a moment's notice to save someone else, there may have been more in it than I gave them credit for.

I guided our guests across the street. When the soldiers returned to our street, they entered our house, but found only my father, my mother and me. It took me years to realize how close to death we had come. Our lives could have ended that day, but evidently the Lord had something else in mind.

Belgium, 1940. I (Janine) was awakened from a deep sleep by some strange noises coming from our kitchen. I could hear voices, some whispering, some quite animated. I recognized one of the voices as belonging to a neighbor. What were they doing at our house so early in the morning?

Then I heard the voice of my father.

Why isn't he at work? I wondered.

Something unusual was going on, but I could not figure out what it was. I decided to go down to find out for myself. When I entered the kitchen and saw the somber faces of the people standing there, I knew something was desperately wrong.

"Mommy, what is going on?" I asked. "Why are you all looking so sad?"

"Janine," she answered, "there are rumors that the Germans are going to invade our country. The Dutch army is mobilizing all the young men to go and fight with the hope that we will push back the Germans."

I was only seven years old and did not fully comprehend all the implications of war. Nevertheless, I felt like my young world was being shattered. My Daddy was leaving us. Would he ever come back? My parents, being Christians, tried to reassure me that the Lord would take care of Daddy and of us.

The following day, before we were ready to take him to the train station, he called our family together to share with us the deep desire of his heart. His mother was working in Brussels as a cook for a baroness; there was no way to let her know that her son was leaving for war. He really wanted to say good-bye to her. So, believing the promise of the Lord that He would give us the desires of our hearts, he prayed and asked the Lord to make it possible.

We left for the train station in Mons. Just as we were ready to say our good-byes, a train pulled in from Brussels. I stood there, watching the people coming out of the train. Suddenly, I couldn't believe my eyes.

"Daddy, look! See who is coming out of the train! Grandma!"

What a reunion! The Lord had given my father the desire of his heart. He had answered his prayer. However, I was really puzzled.

"Daddy," I asked, "the Lord answers prayers, right?"

"Yes, He does."

"But Daddy, when you were asking the Lord to make it possible to see Grandma, she was already sitting in the train. How did she know she had to come home?"

His answer was a revelation to me, a young girl, seven years old.

"The Lord answers prayers, but sometimes He answers even before you ask because He knows what you need," he told us. I learned that day about trusting the Lord for all our needs. At the time I did not know that the Lord would call me to be a missionary, but I believe that through all those experiences during the war He was preparing me for His service.

My father's leaving left a big void in our lives. We missed him greatly. When would we see him again? Would he be safe if fighting broke out? We had no answers to those questions, but we knew we could commit him and his safety into the Lord's hands.

People in our village started to panic, fearing the coming of the Germans. Many decided to flee to the South of France. My maternal grandmother and some of her family members had already evacuated to France. Soon we were about the only ones left in the neighborhood. We did not want to be left behind, so we decided to leave too, accompanied by my father's parents. We did not own a car; in fact, few people in Belgium did at that time. So we loaded some of our belongings on a bicycle and left. We must have been quite a sight, but we didn't care; we just wanted to get to a safe place.

We walked for several hours and finally arrived at the French border where we hoped to catch a train. As we were walking on a dirt road, a huge bull barred our way. My mother was wearing a red coat that must have attracted the animal, because he started to charge toward her. My mother, being quite fearless, took off her coat and shooed the beast away. Believe it or not, he took off in a hurry, and we never saw him again. We often teased Mother about that, telling her that we would enter her in a rodeo where she would have a good chance of winning!

With such poor means of travel, Mother got impatient and declared, "I am quitting; let's go back home." We all agreed.

This proved to be a good move, because only three weeks later Belgium capitulated to the Germans, and my father returned. Having Dad with us again gave us such a safe feeling. Our hearts were full of gratitude to the Lord for His protection on Daddy's life.

The war was the beginning of four difficult years for me as I experienced for the first time danger, lack of food and lack of many other things I had always taken for granted. My parents, who had only been my age when World War I had broken out, had already experienced all this. Quite a few times they would tell me of their experiences and how the Lord had seen them through those hard times. The One who had protected them was still the same Lord.

One night we were awakened by a siren warning the village of approaching planes. We all got up and ran for safety to a nearby meadow. The neighbors were already gathered there. People who had never prayed in their lives started to pray, some to Mary, others to Joseph or St. Christopher. We prayed to the Lord. The planes flew overhead and dropped some bombs over a nearby town but far enough away so that we were not in danger. A few times after that we ran for cover, but the bombings became such a common practice that we just stayed in bed.

Even though such threats were always there, the danger for us came from another source. My father joined the Resistance, a secret organization composed of Belgian men who intended to sabotage the German regime. His life was in constant danger; if he were found out, it could mean deportation to a concentration camp. To my great delight, he let me in on the secret because he needed my help. I was eight years old then, and like my father, I had the spirit of adventure. He was at that time working in a coal mine in a neighboring village. Regularly, he would bring home sticks of dynamite; however, what he planned to do with them, he never revealed to me, but I could guess.

Sometimes we would hear of bridges and railways being blown up. Putting two and two together, I understood what the dynamite was used for. My father was just the middleman—he never took part in the actual action. But it was dangerous for him to carry the explosives himself, so he would ask me to go and meet him at his work. He would then pass on the sticks to me to carry home in my little school bag. We never walked together in case the Germans might stop and search him. Once I got home, I would go outside to a shed and put the incriminating material in some old shoes. My mother was unaware of what I was doing, but she was intrigued by my frequent trips to the shed. One day she followed me.

Our secret was out! My father had some explaining to do, and he did not get away with it. My mother got very angry and aimed some old shoes at my father's head. She made Dad promise that he would never again involve me in this kind of dangerous work. So, to my chagrin, that was the end of my adventures.

Not for my father though!

One afternoon, he came home with some disturbing news. The resistance group with which he was working had decided to send a group of Belgian men to the South of France to work on a German submarine base. My father, being a true patriot with a strong sense of adventure, did not hesitate to accept the challenge. Of course, we understood that this job wasn't to help the German cause but to spy on them.

A few weeks later, he left. Our hearts were very heavy and anxious. We knew the dangers he would face if the Nazis found out what he was doing. If they were caught spying, there would be no pity for them. While he was gone, my mother and I went through hard times, trying to make ends meet on a small budget.

One evening as we were eating our evening meal that was quite meager but enough to satisfy us, suddenly, I realized that all the food was gone—and so was our money. I started to cry.

"Mommy, what are we going to eat tomorrow?"

"I don't know," she answered, "but the Lord will provide. Let's ask Him to help us." She prayed and reminded the Lord of His promises that He would never fail us or forsake us.

That evening, as we were starting to get ready for bed, we heard a knock at the door. These were dangerous times, so we hesitated to open the door at night. But the person was quite persistent and kept on knocking. Finally, my mother inquired who it was. We were relieved to hear that it was a man from the Brethren Church we were attending.

"Don't you know that it is dangerous to go out at night?" Mother asked. "What are you doing out so late?"

The brother explained that he was getting ready to go to bed when the Lord told him that we had a need and that he was supposed to go to our house. He wasn't about to go out at that time of the night, so he told the Lord he would do it the next morning. He went to bed, but the Lord must have nudged him persuasively, because he said, "All right, Lord, I will go now."

He was the answer to our prayer. He gave us some help, and we had enough food for several days. In the meantime, we were without news from my dad. What was happening to him? Was he still alive? What else could we do but pray for his safety? Friends from the church and family members who were also burdened for him started asking the Lord to bring him back safely.

One night, we heard a voice softly calling my mother's name.

"Debora, open the door, it's me."

Father looked as if he had gone through a fire, his clothes were in rags, and he was very thin. After many hugs and many tears, he described what had happened.

The Germans at the submarine base became suspicious of this group of Belgian men and started to watch them closely. They received information that the next day they were to be shipped to Germany to work in a prison camp. My father could not really explain what had happened. But the Lord had opened a door, and he had been able to escape. His friends were sent to Germany; some came back, others never did.

June 1944. D-Day! The day we had longed for had finally arrived. It was hard to believe that after four years of deprivation and danger we would finally be free. The news came over the air that the Allies had pushed back the German troops. This was good news! In only a matter of days, the American troops would be arriving in our village. A deafening noise woke us early one morning as military tanks rolled down our cobblestone street. Along with the neighbors, we all went out to welcome our liberators. We could not contain our joy; everyone started dancing and hugging the men who had left their country to fight for our freedom.

One huge middle-aged black American came to me with tears streaming down his face, picked me up, threw me up in the air and gave me a big hug. Was he remembering a child my age he had left behind? I will never find out, but this incident left a lasting impression on me. There was a language barrier (I couldn't speak English, and he didn't know French), but we both understood the language of love.

As the tanks rolled by, the soldiers gave out chewing gum and chocolate. This was my introduction to chewing gum—I was not impressed by the taste. But the chocolate was a different story! After four years, I had forgotten how it tasted. I made it last as long as I could.

Eventually, life returned to normal, and we were soon to forget all the hardships we had gone through. One thing we never forgot, though, was the faithfulness of the Lord. He had proved Himself true to His promises in protecting us and providing for all our needs. He had not failed us!

Endnotes

1. Corrie ten Boom with John and Elizabeth Sherrill, *The Hiding Place* (Uhrichsville, OH: Barbour & Co., 1987).

2. Cornelius Ryan, *A Bridge Too Far* (New York: Simon and Schuster, YEAR), n.p.

2

The Call

My call had been clear and undeniable, although slow in taking shape. I had always considered myself to be a Christian since I had grown up in the Christian Reformed Church of which my parents were members. My three brothers and I would never have considered breaking the obligatory church-going rule, at least on Sunday mornings. It is true that during my almost two-year-long cure for tuberculosis of the lungs, which I had contracted as a result of the period of starvation the western part of Holland went through during the last eight months of the war, I had drifted away from my Christian heritage. Prayer and Bible reading had not been part of my daily routine while resting before the open window of my upstairs bedroom. My life had been filled to the brim with classical music, reading and playing chess. But during those days, the Lord planted a seed in my heart and mind which later led to my conversion.

I had read a novel by a Dutch author, Jan de Hartog, telling the story of a drunkard in the city of Rotterdam who had been picked out of the gutter by the Salvation Army. He was gloriously saved, and his life was completely transformed. So also was the prostitute he lived with. The two of them eventually married and served as missionaries under the auspices of the Salvation Army to what was then called the Dutch East Indies, now known as Indonesia. The reading of this book awakened in me the thought that the gospel could bring about such life-changing transformations. I had never seen Christians like that, but I began to conceive of the possibility that they might exist.

When I was allowed to go back to school at the age of seventeen, I had to start high school over again. Meanwhile, some of my friends in school had found the Lord at the home of a pastor of the Dutch Reformed Church. I didn't like the smell of holiness that hung around them, and when they invited me for a retreat I looked for excuses so I could say I was not free to go. That was December 1949. However, at their insistence, I promised that I would go with them to the next retreat at Easter, 1950.

When Easter came around, my friends did too. They even offered to pay my way. As I was led away, I made up my mind that this John Schultz would come back the same way he had gone. Nobody was going to talk me into anything. Was I in for a surprise! When I arrived at the retreat, I found myself surrounded by Christians such as I had read about in the novel—and they were my peers! I tried to brush off their obvious joy by telling myself that they must be faking it. But that did not hold up. I had to admit that they had something I didn't have.

During those days, I came to understand that the way to receive what they had was to ask Jesus to come into my heart. Considering that matter, I realized how dirty I was inside. My heart was full of things I felt ashamed of, things I wouldn't want anyone to know about, not even the Lord. So I told God I was sorry, but that He would have to stay outside. During one of the sermons, however, I forgot my resolve, and just by way of experiment, I left the door ajar, thinking I could quickly close it if things went too far. The Lord directly put His foot in the door and flooded my soul with a joy that I had never experienced before; I never even suspected such a thing existed.

My first reaction was: "Oh, no! Now I am going to be exposed! He will go through the filth and hold up the dirty laundry of my life for everyone to see. 'You see what kind of a guy this John Schultz actually is,' He would say for all to hear." I did not hear a voice from heaven, but I knew the Lord was saying to me: "Don't you understand, John? Those things you are so ashamed about are exactly the sins Jesus died for at the cross. I am not even going to talk about them anymore." For the first time in my life, I felt thoroughly loved. I felt a load slide off my shoulders, and I began to walk straight and free.

Finally, on my twenty-first birthday, I graduated from high school. At that time a team from Youth For Christ International visited the city of Haarlem. With some friends from school, I volunteered to help set up a tent in the center of town and to give out in-

THE CALL

vitations for the rallies. One evening, I was on my way back to the tent when I looked over my shoulder and saw some young people hanging over the railing of a bridge in the distance. A little voice inside told me to go and invite them, but I didn't feel like walking all the way back, so I went into the tent.

I didn't feel happy, but I thought that I would soon be swept off my feet as usual when the singing started. This did not happen, and I felt very miserable. I realized that something was wrong with my obedience to the Lord. I had obeyed Him when I felt like it, and when I was not in the mood, I ignored Him. When I looked up to the Lord in prayer and promised Him that I would henceforth obey whether I felt like it or not, it was as if I was struck by lightning. I understood that the Lord wanted me to go into full-time service.

This was a most upsetting discovery. I had my own plans for my life: I wanted to become a teacher. Going into full-time service seemed to mean giving up my dream. At the end of the service, I went forward to confirm my call, and the pastor prayed with me. At home, I told my father, and he became very upset.

"I don't want you to become a backwoods evangelist," he told me. "You just graduated from high school, you must find a job and bring in some money."

Whom was I going to obey? I prayed and read my Bible. The only answer I received seemed to be: "Children, obey your parents." I was twenty-one years old, but the text did not specify an age limit. So I asked the Lord to help me find a job, and then to overrule my father when He saw fit. God did overrule my father, but I did not like the way He did it.

My mother had been ill for years and, in September 1952, she passed away. At that time, my father was apparently in good health. But soon after my mother's death, he fell ill, and the doctor confirmed that he had terminal lung cancer. He died four months after my mother. I suddenly realized that there was nobody to whom I had to give account to, so I began to look into the possibility of getting some formal training to serve the Lord.

Before long I found myself at the Brussels Bible Institute in Belgium. But what was I going to do with my diploma? I was told that I had three years to ponder that question. Sometime during my first semester, a French-speaking church in Belgium held its yearly convention in the building where the Bible school was located. The last service was a missionary rally. I remember only an illustration one of the preachers used. He told about a man who had surrendered his life to the Lord without any strings attached. He said: "If You send me to the North Pole, I will go. If You send me to the equator, I will go there. If You tell me to stay at home, I will stay at home. If You take my body and put me in bed for the rest of my life, as an invalid, I will accept that. You may do with me what You want." That really hit me! I knew that I had never made such an act of surrender to God. I raised my hand at the invitation and told the Lord that I handed Him a blank sheet of paper for Him to write on whatever He wanted. I wasn't even going to think what that might be.

About two weeks later, I attended another missionary rally, this time in a Flemish-speaking church. A missionary from Holland, who had been working in

THE CALL

Indonesia under The Christian and Missionary Alliance, showed slides of the Alliance work in Dutch New Guinea (now Irian Jaya, Indonesia). I had never heard of The Christian and Missionary Alliance, but I recognized one young lady from my hometown on the slides.

The missionaries had landed with an amphibian plane on the water of the Baliem River, risking their lives in the process, to bring the gospel to the Dani people who were still living in the Stone Age. I had never seen such dedication, and I was deeply moved. That evening I knelt beside my bed and told the Lord that I would go to New Guinea if that was what He wanted me to do. When I received no clear answer, the matter became the main subject of my daily prayers. Soon I realized that I had never prayed for missionaries, and if I were to join the missionary ranks, I should do something about that. So I made Dutch New Guinea my prayer project. Every day I spent five or ten minutes in prayer specifically for that faraway country. This stimulated me to read all I could find about what went on there. I worked on that project for the remainder of my three years at the Brussels Bible Institute.

As the time for graduation approached, I contacted the missionary who had kindled the desire in me. Rev. William Könemann had spent the war years in a Japanese concentration camp. When the war ended, he was sent back to Holland, broken in body, but not in spirit. He recuperated somewhat, but never enough to return to the mission field. He struggled with this, saying: "Lord, You called me to be a missionary; why do I have to stay at home?" The way to go back never opened up. Finally, Brother Könemann accepted the will of God, but under one condition, that He would send ten people to go in his place. I did not know this when I applied, nor did I not understand why my application was rejected. I was told that the Alliance would not send single men to Dutch New Guinea.

Since I was sure that the Lord wanted me to go to Dutch New Guinea, I concluded that He wanted me to get married first. But how would I find a partner for life who would be willing to go to Dutch New Guinea and who would have received the same call God had given me in a Bible school where dating was forbidden? God, however, had His own unique way of bringing Janine and me together. Within a few months after I was initially turned down by the Alliance, we were engaged, accepted as candidates, married and sent out! But that is another chapter.

October 15, 1957: I am sick in bed at the home of my brother Rudolph. My fever went up to 105 degrees as a result of the smallpox vaccination I received a few days ago at a clinic in Amsterdam. I failed to receive this vaccination as a child during a period when the municipal government of Haarlem decided that vaccinations were no longer needed for children to enter school. Now my sins caught up with me and, being an adult, the vaccine hit me much harder than it would have had I received it in my childhood. Rudolph's family physician was kind enough to make a house call and suggested that some aspirin would make life more bearable for me.

October 18: Back in Belgium, at the home of my parents-in-law where Janine and I have been bivouacking since our wedding, awaiting our departure for New Guinea. Most of our time is spent in purchasing our outfit and packing two small crates that will have to be taken to the harbor in Amsterdam prior to our embarkation on December 1. A dear lady in Holland has donated a small pump organ that is in very good condition. It will have to take the place of a piano. The only kind of my classical music I will be able to play on it will be Bach. I am very excited, to the point that often I don't know where to turn. My brave wife seems to be much more level-headed than I am, and she behaves as if preparing for a trip to the other side of the world and a four-year stint in the tropics is something she has often faced before in her life.

November 17: I have delivered our outfit at the dock, from which it will be put on board the *MS Billiton*, a Dutch freighter with passenger accommodations, that will take us to Dutch New Guinea. I need another inoculation at the clinic. When the male nurse pokes the needle in my arm, he asks where I am going. "To the Wissel Lakes, in New Guinea," I answer. "Nice," he retorts, "but rough country. Good luck." That afternoon, Janine and I met my aunt who spent several years of her life in Indonesia. One of her lifetime friends, with whom she worked together over the years, casts a searching glance at me as if she wants to analyze my character and perseverance. "The Wissel Lakes! I have been there. You won't last a year!" So much for encouragement!

November 30: Janine's family has accompanied us to Haarlem, where we all spent the night for our departure the next morning. I feel too excited to be melancholy. It will be much harder for Janine to say good-bye to her parents than for me who has only one brother left in Holland.

December 1: This is the great day! We had frost during the night. In beautiful clear winter weather we drive to the harbor. A cold wind hits us in the face when we arrive at the dock. The captain of the ship welcomes us as two of the twelve passengers who will be on board. He mentions in passing that he read in the local newspaper about our farewell service at the Evangelical Chapel in Haarlem. I compliment him on his being so up-to-date, and he says that he makes a point of knowing all he can about his passengers.

We are shown to our cabin. All passenger accommodations on a freighter are first class. Janine's father, mother and her younger brother, Jean-Marie, accompany us on board. Then comes the ringing of the bell indicating that departure time has arrived. We separate amid many tears. Leaning over the railing, two decks above the quay, we see the family standing, shivering in the cold. Janine's parents, my brother and his family, the friends who took me into their home after my parents died and a friend from high school comprise our farewell committee. One of the sailors throws off the hawsers with which the ship was moored, and a small pilot boat starts pulling us toward the North Sea Canal on our way to the ocean, to Dutch New Guinea, to the other end of the world.

About six weeks later, on January 12, 1958, we disembarked from the Dutch freighter *Billiton* on which my bride, Janine, and I had spent a six-week honeymoon. We had arrived in Manokwari, a city on the Bird's Head area of Dutch New Guinea. Here, this Dutchman from the flatlands beheld his first high mountain. It was an overwhelming experience. This was the land that had been in our thoughts and prayers for the last three years.

The sweltering heat hit us hard. Unaccustomed to such a climate, we made the mistake of going for a walk in the middle of the day as we would do in Western Europe. We soon learned to change our habits. A friendly missionary couple, working with TEAM, took us in while we waited for the MAF airplane to pick us up and fly us to our destination, the Wissel Lakes. Three days later, the plane, with its pilot, Pablo Pontier, arrived.

Very early in the morning, before daybreak, Pablo drove us in a Jeep to the little local airport. We pulled up in front of the smallest aircraft on the tarmac. I had never flown, nor had I ever even been close to an airplane. Boarding a slightly larger one would have been more reassuring. Janine got in the back, and I strapped myself into the copilot's seat. The engine roared, and we took off. A few feet off the ground, I had the clear impression that we were not moving. It flashed through my mind that ours might be the shortest missionary career on record! However, the pilot seemed composed, the plane gained altitude, and soon we were over the deep blue water of the Pacific Ocean.

About one-and-a-half hours later, we cleared the Geelvink Bay, and Pablo pointed out the newest MAF air base, called Nabire. Little did we know how large Nabire would loom in our lives in later years. After leaving Nabire behind us, a strange picture presented itself to our view. In the distance, above the level where one would expect to see the horizon, was a large body of water. It looked like an optical illusion, as if we were looking up to the water level. The view was breathtaking.

We also flew through a region of high mountains with impressive walls rising above the little airplane on either side. The sky was clear. Only a few puffs of clouds clung to the mountaintops.

About twenty-one years before we arrived, a young lieutenant of the Dutch Marines had flown over the spot where we were flying and made the discovery of his life. In old Dutch Archives we found the following report:

> It was December 31, 1936, when Lieutenant Wissel received the order to make a flight to the south coast, where one of the cartographers was in trouble. During this historic flight the pilot discovered a large lake in the heart of the Bird's Head [actually this was not the Bird's Head but the Neck of the Bird], which had never been spotted before. From the onset the weather was beautiful, with only minimum cloud coverage.

The airplane passed the coastline and the small strip of beach. The mountain range with a skyline of over six thousand feet stood in sharp contrast with the clear blue sky behind. The twin-engine airplane had to top those mountains. The aircraft droned over the uninhabited mountains below. The jungle underneath was green, cut through with silver mountain streams and rivers. A few solitary parrots that were scared by the plane were the only signs of life. Against the dark green of the forest, the mountains stood off even darker. It was a somber, depressing, and wild landscape.

One mountain was spotted that dominated the whole scene. From the middle to the top, it was devoid of vegetation. No trace of green marked the top. The pilot immediately baptized this landmark The Bare Mountain. The aircraft flew over one of the wildest places on earth, heading toward the heart of the island, and toward the lakes. Cloudless days are rare on this island of eternal rain and fog. Suddenly the men saw something white glittering below them. In front, between deep mountain gorges, hidden behind massive mountain walls, they saw three small pieces of glistering silver. These were the lakes, and they lay in the heart of stone of the island.

The twin-engine craft lowered its altitude to reach the lakes that were about six thousand feet above sea level. Wissel steered straight for the largest of the three. With cut-down engines, the plane dove to about 120 feet above the water level. The men saw a smooth polished mirror, glistening in the sun, reflecting the blue sky above and the mountain walls that surrounded it. They saw more: canoes . . . thirty . . . forty small canoes . . . and in each of them three or four men were seated. They were small, naked people. The airplane skimmed low over the lake, and there was not much time for observation. In the few moments that watching was allowed, they tried to take in as much as they could, but the time was very short. The fuel supply was limited, and the airplane had to fly on.

Wissel considered the possibility of landing on the water, but that risk would be too great to take. Taking off from an altitude of approximately six thousand feet would have been hazardous. So, the crew utilized the time by watching sharply and clicking their cameras. In each of the canoes they saw a large kind of round net with a bamboo hoop on top of it. The three little people were probably fishing. [Later, it was discovered that the lakes did not harbor any fish, only shrimp.]

The arrival of the airplane brought about indescribable consternation among the men in the canoes. They froze and sat like stone statues in their boats, staring in terror at the huge bird that had come over the mountains, flew toward them, and was about to fall on top of them. They were petrified. This terrible, roaring demon had come from the sky to fall upon them, barely a few feet above the water of the lake. Some men jumped overboard and hid under the water surface. Others curled up in their canoes.

At this point the crew realized that they had forgotten to haul in their radio aerial lead wire. The one-hundred-foot-long steel cable with a copper bullet at the end swished over the heads of the little black people in the canoes. The aerial was taken in as fast as possible. The plane circled the eastern part of the lake a few times and surveyed a large valley that narrowed toward the east. They saw a rather large hut, with a roof covering made out of tall grass. In the vicinity, gardens were observed, walled in by stone fences about three feet high. The gardens were cut through with small paths, which gave the impression of a large tablet of chocolate divided up in smaller squares. Wissel turned toward the south. Then the men saw a second lake, much smaller than the first one, and behind that a third lake. They had the impression that the level of those lakes were higher than that of the bigger one.[1]

Thirty minutes later, we entered the pass to the Wissel Lakes, and shortly thereafter we landed on the small grass airfield of Obano, which was the only landing strip in the area at that time.

We were familiar with the name Obano. About one year earlier, angry natives had attacked the mission station in Obano, killing an Indonesian couple who were teachers and several Indonesian children. They had also demolished the mission airplane that was on the airfield. (See *Out There Beyond Beyond*, by Edward Ulrich with Larry Lake, #24 in the Jaffray Collection of Missionary Portraits.) Our Alliance missionary, Elze Stringer, had escaped with her life because she had crossed the lake to spend the weekend in Enarotali. We had heard that everything was quiet now, but this did not make us less apprehensive when our plane touched down at the very spot where the rebellion had started.

We were immediately surrounded by scores of natives. We had seen their pictures, and we knew that their dress code defied description. The women wore grass skirts, and the men had a poor excuse for a pair of slacks called a *koteka* or penis gourd. We thought we knew what we were in for, but we didn't. Handshakes were unknown among the Kapauku tribespeople; they snap fingers. This we knew, but we were not prepared for the hands that had never been in contact with soap and water. Were these the people God had sent us to in order to tell them about His love? Could we learn to love them? We desperately needed God's help.

One of the young missionaries met us at the plane. Bill Stieglitz had crossed the lake, coming from Enarotali in a wooden canoe with an outboard motor. The boat was docked about forty minutes' walk from the airstrip. Several men hoisted our luggage on their shoulders and followed us on our walk to the shore. Then suddenly, the air was filled with what sounded to us like war whoops. Pictures of last year's uprising flashed through our minds, but Bill assured us that this was the people's normal way to give utterance to a joyous occasion.

The crossing took about an hour. From the pictures we had seen we recognized the mountain which protrudes like the Rock of Gibraltar in the lake at Enarotali. All of a sudden we were in those pictures that we had studied in preparation for our departure. We had arrived at the place to which the Lord had called us.

A group of seven missionaries welcomed us at the landing in Enarotali. Among them were Walter and Viola Post, the first missionary couple to arrive at the Wissel Lakes before World War II. Although the Mission board representative, Ken Troutman, was not present, we were to stay with the Troutmans for the time being until the log cabin that would be our first home would be ready. Vida Troutman greeted us warmly. That night we had our first taste of life in the Stone Age. We went to our bedroom with a kerosene lamp, no electricity being available. As soon as we entered the room, hundreds of cockroaches scurried away.

"You mean we will have to sleep with roaches?" Janine shrieked.

"I suppose they won't come on the bed," I tried to reassure her. She was not convinced, so I went downstairs to ask Vida how to counter this invasion. With a kind smile, she told me that roaches were a common entity in New Guinea and that most people had learned to live with them. Since we were both dead tired, and since there were no other options, we closed our eyes, hoping the roaches would do the same.

I was shocked! This was what is scientifically known as culture shock. From the Western hemisphere, where we had been surrounded by familiar faces, conditions and other little things that had reaffirmed our identity and had made us feel useful and important, we had been transferred into a different world. I felt as if I were no longer on the same planet. I was an adult, fluent in my own language, but nobody could understand me here. Kenny Troutman, ten years old, spoke the native language fluently. How embarrassing it was to have to call Kenny twenty times a day to ask him what people were saying! How deflating for my ego when, at times, Kenny didn't feel like being helpful! I felt like I was back to being a two-year-old.

The Mission had laid down the rule that novices had to spend eight hours a day in language study. There were no organized classes and no professional tutors, but Marion Doble, the Mission linguist, who had reduced the tribal language to writing and had just finished the translation of the New Testament, had prepared language material for our study. A student at the Bible school was assigned to help us with reading. Unfortunately, he did not feel that it was proper for him to correct a white person, so he agreed with every mispronunciation we made. The discipline to sit down and study was hard. One of our leaders sent a letter to the U.S. headquarters expressing doubt that I would ever learn the language.

One complicating factor was that the only connection with the outside world was the MAF airplane which landed at the airfield of Obano, ten miles across the lake. The plane had to be met by someone, and so the newly arrived missionary was chosen to ferry the wooden canoe with outboard motor across, wait for the plane, load the boat with all the stuff that came in and go back to Enarotali. In order to accomplish this, I had to leave Enarotali before the sun came up and before the weather could be checked to see if it was a good day for flying.

Since poor weather often cleared up later in the morning, I was instructed that I had to wait till noon before I could call it a day. By that time, the wind had increased, whipping up waves that could bring water into the canoe. None of this was conducive to language study, but it did provide opportunity to mix with people away from the station. I began to pick up words that were not even in Marion Doble's language course!

As sounds began to make sense, and words began to come, it was shocking to discover that the people's concept of truth was quite different from what I had grown up with. I began to realize that, in our Western society, even atheists have an understanding of truth and of man's obligation toward it. Christianity had influenced our society and molded the thinking and behavior even of people who did not acknowledge the truth of the gospel or the existence of God. But these Stone Age tribespeople had never been under this influence. God was a vague concept for them, without any bearing upon the realities of everyday life. Spiritual actuality was expressed in defending oneself against the influences of evil spirits. The best way to do this was to deceive those spirits and lead them into thinking that they had mistaken the identity of the person they were attacking. Truth, therefore, had little or no practical value. It was shocking to realize that even Christians would tell lies with a straight face and cheerfully try to cheat someone out of his possessions.

All the props upon which we had built the security and comfort of our daily lives in the West were knocked out from under us. At least the apostle Paul had had some common ground with the people he tried to win for Christ! Kipling stated a great truth when he wrote: "East is East, and West is West, and never the twain shall meet." The only common ground we had with these Stone Age people was the fact that we had the same Creator who loved the world so much that He gave His only Son, so that whoever would believe in Him would not perish but have eternal life.

Unless these people could believe, they would perish. That was the reason we found ourselves in this different world as if on another other planet. Our call had been clear and undeniable.

Endnote

1. Translated from the Dutch *Jungle Pimpernel* by Antony van Kampen.

3

Stone Age Shock

When we left Belgium and Holland, we were newly married. Since the freighter we were boarding had no doctor on board, I had to sign a document stating that my wife was not pregnant. I had signed in good faith, but after one week on the ocean, we began to have doubts about Janine's seasickness, since it seemed to be limited strictly to the morning hours. A French doctor in Djibouti, East Africa, the first harbor where we were allowed off board, confirmed our suspicions.

We tried to keep the matter secret, but an observant female passenger came to Janine, and asked with a frankness typical of the Dutch, "Are you pregnant?" We confirmed her surmise and swore her to secrecy.

August 20, 1958, Ruth Ann was born at 7:30 p.m. Finally, the months of waiting had come to an end. The Dutch doctor in Enarotali came to our little log cabin as Janine's labor pains increased in frequency. He tried to locate the bag that he had sent ahead with one of the male Papuan nurses from the hospital. We finally found it in front of the house that belonged to Marion Doble who was single and blissfully unaware of what was going on!

Sitting on a chair beside the bed on which Janine was going through her hours of pain, I reflected on the past several months. Typical of almost every evening in the interior of Irian Jaya, the rain was pounding on our tin roof as the crisp coolness of the mountains began to descend upon us. Nights were always cool, sometimes even cold, at this altitude of 5,600 feet above sea level. We were about to have our first child. How had we come to this great day in our lives?

My mind went back to a dormitory room at the Brussels Bible Institute in Belgium. About one-and-a-half years earlier, I had sat at the edge of my bed pondering what lay ahead. I had told the Lord during the impasse in my application to the Alliance that I looked forward to getting married, but that I desperately needed His help to find out whom He had in mind for me. I had been in love before. I knew the curious feeling in the pit of my stomach and how it could blur my reasoning power. Falling in love ought not to be my first priority, but knowing the Lord's plan certainly was.

I prayed one of the most curious prayers ever prayed by mortal man: "Lord, please keep me from falling in love!" The Lord honored my request! I managed to control my emotions, but I did keep my eyes open. The regulations of the school prevented my doing extensive research, until I realized that every school has an appropriate place for research—the library!

One evening, in search of a book, I bumped into Janine Baleine. Since we had sat in the same classroom the previous year, I already knew her quite well. I liked her. As innocently as I could, I asked her if she had ever considered going to Dutch New Guinea as a missionary. For some reason, she saw straight through me and declared herself unwilling to discuss the subject then and there.

But three days later, we found each other again behind the bookshelves in the library. She then confessed something to me that I now consider a sheer miracle. Yes, the Lord had called her long before I broached the subject, and she had prayed: "Please Lord, don't let me go alone!"

We felt like two work crews must feel when, starting from opposite sides, they dig a tunnel through a mountain and meet in the middle. If this wasn't the Lord's doing, what was it? I canceled the prayer about not falling in love—and the cancellation went into effect immediately! The leadership of the school approved of our engagement, as did Janine's parents. We both applied to the Alliance, and this time we were both accepted.

When we graduated in June 1957, the Alliance told us that we would have to spend two years doing home service before they would send us out. The status of our finances, or rather the lack of them, made us decide to wait for marriage until we had advanced well into those two years. But barely one month after graduation, Rev. Könemann phoned and asked if we could possibly leave for Dutch New Guinea on the boat that would leave in September, two months later.

"We're not even married yet!" I exclaimed.

"You better get married soon then," came the rather laconic answer. Well, we didn't make the September boat, but we were married in that month.

Those reflections forced themselves upon me as Janine's labor pains increased and the doctor with a Dutch nurse prepared themselves for action. This was a completely new experience for me, and I tried to control my excitement. But when Ruthy's first little cry was heard, I sat down on the edge of the bed and cried my eyes out. I was so overwhelmed by this miracle that when I later went downstairs to tell Vida about our new daughter, she thought that I had lost my wife and newborn child.

We were the first newly arrived missionaries to have a baby in Enarotali. I was the proudest father who ever lived, and, in my mind at least, Janine was the best woman ever to give birth to a child. The miracle was repeated three more times in the next several years. God brought us to Dutch New Guinea, and He blessed us with children. One of the students of the tribal Bible school who helped us in and around the house looked at our little baby the next morning and declared that "Glootee" (he tried to say "Ruthy," but his native tongue made no allowances for the "r"), had a white man's nose. Obviously, this set her apart from all the other babies around.

When Ruthy was only a few weeks old, we moved to our first assignment, the little village of Gakokebo, at the edge of Lake Tigi, the most southern of the three Wissel Lakes. Lake Tigi was a beautiful place. Our spacious house, constructed of rough-hewn boards, was less than 100 yards from the shore of the lake. There was a small plywood boat with outboard motor at our disposal, and the lake abounded with sweet water shrimp which the local population was eager to trade for a cup full of glass beads.

In Gakokebo, we were immediately submerged in a great variety of responsibilities without any kind of introduction. The Alliance had begun a modest elementary education program which was subsidized by the Dutch government. The Dutch simply transferred their educational program from the homeland to their colony, adhering to the principle that education was primarily the responsibility of the parents. The government subsidized programs that were instituted by the parents as long as they met the accepted standards.

Since the Stone-Age Kapauku parents were quite unconcerned about their children's need for elementary education, it was decreed that the Mission Societies in the areas under the control of the Dutch government would serve as proxy parents. In the Wissel Lakes area, this meant that the Catholic Mission and The Christian and Missionary Alliance received a certain amount of government subsidy to carry out the task of educating the native children.

This involved, of course, extensive administrative work. All communications with the Dutch Department of Education were in Dutch, which the American missionary previously in charge of the program had not mastered. So upon my arrival on the field, a file cabinet with all the documents pertaining to the program was dumped in my lap without any word of explanation. It had never been understood by anyone in our Mission.

The Catholic Mission, however, which was manned for the most part by Dutch priests, knew what they were doing and took full advantage of our ignorance. School supervision was almost a full-time job, as was oversight of the Tigi district which had more than a dozen churches with their pastors, plus the local Continuation School, which was the higher level of elementary education, at which I taught about twenty hours per week. We also had to continue our Kapauku language study and try to communicate with the Indonesian teachers in the elementary schools. If there ever was a sink or swim situation, this was it. The Lord taught us to swim, though not without problems.

The fact that our house was in the very middle of a native village made language learning easier. Before the end of six months in Gakokebo, I was able to preach locally, and Janine began a ministry with the women who came and sat in our yard learning Bible verses, singing choruses and listening to short Bible messages in their language played on a record player.

Soon we were also introduced to the urgent medical needs of the people in the village. The first occurrence was a baby, only a few months old, who had rolled into the fire in the middle of the night. The Kapauku live in small huts made of hewn boards which are tied together with rattan vine and covered with a roof of tree bark. The floor is about three feet above the ground, and in the middle is a fireplace built with rocks. Since the nights in the mountains are cold, people sleep on mats around the fire. Babies are put on top of their carrying nets close to the fire. Frequently toddlers roll over in the middle of the night and burn themselves.

This child's mother brought him to us about two weeks after the accident had occurred. All his hair had been singed off, the wound was badly infected, and the only covering was some leaves that were supposed to promote healing. The stench was overwhelming. We both worked on the poor child, who screamed loudly as together we cleaned his wound and bandaged his head.

When the people of the village realized that our medical assistance met with some measure of success, patients started coming on a daily basis—and in a rather disorganized manner—at any time they wished. We tried to create some order and to set up clinic hours. Unfortunately, neither Janine nor I had ever had any medical training. The nearest medical help was the hospital in Enarotali, about twenty miles away. The Dutch doctors were willing to help, but they were not omnipresent. Sporadically, they crisscrossed the region, holding campaigns to eradicate yaws and to treat people who came with various complaints.

When one of the doctors came to Gakokebo, he set up clinic for a day and spent the night with us. He was very sympathetic to what we were trying to do, and he left a supply of medications for the most common ailments we were likely to encounter. He checked the Papuan teacher of the elementary school and diagnosed chronic asthma with a bronchial infection. He prescribed a series of penicillin shots, leaving ten bottles with me, plus a reusable syringe and needles. The closest I had ever come to a syringe was when a doctor gave me shots of penicillin to combat blood poisoning in Brussels. I had never laid my hand on any myself.

The doctor was quite confident, however, that I could do it. So every evening, I went to see Mr. Rumaseb to inject him with penicillin. I don't know whose prayers prevailed, his or mine, but I'm sure we both prayed fervently—and we both survived.

In giving out medicines, our eyes were opened to needs that went beyond the physical. Much suffering was self-inflicted and related to the superstitious demands the culture of the tribe imposed. In the minds of the people, there was no such thing as a physical cause for an ailment; all sickness had a spiritual basis. Dysentery was the result of a spell cast upon a person. Our pills were, therefore, not mere chemical substances used to kill microbes, but soul-stuff that was stronger than the magic that caused the sickness. Injection needles were considered to be the ultimate in spiritual power. If one shot of oil-based penicillin could clear up the ugly painful sores of yaws, then it was powerful spirit-stuff.

Some of the folk medicine had tragic consequences. When a loved one died, he or she had to be mourned properly. An inadequate expression of grief could cause the spirit of the deceased to return to the family and cause crops to fail, pigs to die and humans to get sick. As an appropriate token of mourning, therefore, joints of fingers would be cut off. The pain and cries of the victim would make the departed one understand how they felt about his death. Treating infected stumps on the fingers of small children was one of the most heartrending experiences in the early days of our work.

Then there were the wounds inflicted as a result of marital disagreements. A husband would frequently beat his wife whenever she was deemed to be insubordinate. Besides loud screams and theatrical demonstrations of anguish, the woman would cut into the bruises caused by her husband's stick. The reason for this was that the swelling was the result of a spirit that was looking for a way out of the body. Opening the door would give instant relief, and when the next day pus would form, this was seen as proof of the presence of the spirit. Initially, we treated several cases that were the result of marital abuse, but later we announced to the people that if they cut in their own bodies, they would have to suffer the consequences. We would withhold treatment.

This medical ministry brought us into good standing with the local population. The people of Lake Tigi had never been unkind to us, but now they started greeting us more cordially than before. Later, when we moved to Kebo in our second term, our medical clinic became a great attraction to the more than 10,000 people who lived around Lake Paniai.

Gakokebo also introduced us more directly to the effects of some tropical diseases. The clear little mountain stream with its delicious cool water brought amoebae into our systems that would eventually endanger our lives and plague us for years to come. Hepatitis laid both of us up for extended periods of time, and various other intestinal parasites made their abode in us.

During our time in Gakokebo, our son John Paul was born. We had to go to Enarotali for the happy event, since no medical help was available where we lived. The time was December 1959. I decided to combine our family affairs with business and organized a seminar for the school teachers of the elementary schools under the jurisdiction of the Alliance. Most of these young men were on loan from a Dutch Mission society which worked mainly in the coastal area. It turned out that many of them were nominal Christians who had never personally responded to the claims of Christ upon their lives. During this seminar, several of them prayed with me and accepted the Lord.

John Paul, or J.P. as he later came to be known, postponed his arrival which had been originally predicted for the week before Christmas. The Dutch doctor who was going to help in the delivery said that he would appreciate it if the baby to be born would allow him to eat his Christmas dinner in peace. Just for the sake of excitement, we sent him a note at mealtime on the day of Christmas, to tell him that everything was quiet in the mother's womb and that we hoped he enjoyed his meal. J.P. waited a full two weeks after his due date until he finally decided that the time had come for him to begin his career in the world.

We called the doctor late in the evening of December 27. Wisely, he decided to spend the night on the couch in the living room, and when he checked Janine with the help of a flashlight at about 4 a.m. the next morning, things went very fast. I received orders to light the kerosene pressure lamp immediately. This took a few minutes longer than the doctor wanted—I will not repeat what he said. Unfortunately, the first word J.P. heard upon entering this world was a Dutch swearword. It made him burst out in a forceful and healthy cry.

At the beginning of our second year in Gakokebo, additional personnel for the Continuation School had been hired. This arrangement freed me to concentrate on the dual functions of overseeing the elementary school program and the churches in the Tigi Lake and Kamu districts. This involved travel, some of it by crossing Lake Tigi in the little boat with an outboard motor, but most of it by foot. The Tigi District was relatively easy to cover since one could cross the lake and walk from the shore to visit the churches or schools, most of which were within a distance of less than one or two hours.

Trekking to the Kamu Valley was another matter. The Kamu itself must have been a large lake in previous centuries, but the water table had slowly gone down to the point that only the small Makamo Lake was left. The rest was reduced to swamp, some of which was rather dangerous to cross. Even on the official jungle trail, I often sank into the mud up to my knees.

My first experience was a trek from Gakokebo to Dogimani, a walk that took nine hours. Janine stayed home since it would have been very difficult to make the trip with two little children. But our dog, Pierre, insisted on coming along. For the first several hours, he would run back and forth over the trail, covering at least two or three times the same distance I walked. But late in the afternoon, Pierre repeatedly fell down exhausted and refused to move. Only when he saw that I was serious in continuing the trip would he follow, dragging his tail behind him. I myself was completely drained by the end of the day. My heart was still pounding the next day, so I decided to rest. The altitude was not helpful for this kind of vigorous exercise.

On the return trip, I decided to visit the church of Bukapa, which was on the shore of Lake Makamo. When our little expedition—two or three carriers, Pierre and I—reached the lake, we were advised to wait for a canoe that would paddle us across. When no canoe showed up after several hours, I disregarded the advice of the local people and announced that we would walk around the lake. I soon regretted my impatient impulse. Pierre often tried to jump from one patch of ground to another, and missed, sinking in the black water. He found he was unable to pull himself ashore, since the ground would break off when he tried to crawl up. I had to pull him out.

Stepping from clump to clump was like trying to walk on a waterbed. The rubbery ground would sink down under our feet and bulge up, indicating that there was very little underneath to hold us up. My carriers, obviously endowed with the gift of encouragement, would tell stories of people who had fallen in between the patches of ground and had never been seen again. This stimulated prayer, and a sweet sense of the Lord's presence soon encompassed us. Once the canoe arrived, piloted by a woman from Bukapa, we boarded. We soon left the lake behind us and entered a small river. It seemed at several points that we had reached our destination since the river appeared to end. Actually, a large floating island obscured the river behind it, but our pilot would take her oar and push it out of the way. So, we arrived at our destination.

The next morning we had an early start, before sunrise, making a beeline to higher ground. Late that afternoon, I arrived at our house which, at that moment, seemed like the most luxurious and comfortable home on earth, where a long hot bush-shower washed off all the mud of the last four or five days. (A bucket is filled with water, attached to a rope and raised up over a beam by pulleys. When the sprayer is opened, the water comes out like a normal shower. Needless to say, it is important to soap and rinse before the water supply is exhausted!)

One day, as our third year on the field was drawing to an end, I was lying on the couch in our living room recovering from hepatitis when we received word that the Bible school in Enarotali would be closed down. Since the Walter Posts were leaving on furlough, there was nobody available to take their place. Janine and I prayed, and we felt clearly that the Lord wanted us to offer ourselves to fill the empty spot. We wrote to the Field Advisory Committee saying that we would be willing to move to Enarotali and teach in the Bible school. The committee agreed, and in November 1960 we moved to Enarotali.

When I had answered the Lord's call for full-time service, I had given up my dream of becoming a teacher. Now the Lord gave it back to me. Some dreams do come true. Teaching we would both joyfully do for the remainder of our lives in Irian Jaya.

4

War—and the Jungle Adventure

Einar Mickelson, one of the first Alliance pioneer missionary explorers in Dutch New Guinea, had started the Kapauku Bible School in Enarotali. In his book, *God Can*, Mickelson chronicles the events of those years:

> It was not long after our return that we were able to get our first Bible school started in the interior (though it was not at first recognized as qualifying for such a name). This school was possible because Paksoal had returned to the interior. He was not only an experienced teacher and mature Christian worker, but he also knew the unwritten language of the people. His contribution to the work and his influence for good upon the people of the interior will be hard to calcu-

late. Later, Ladjang was appointed to help Paksoal in the work of the Bible school.[1]

Thus, on August 3, 1948, a crude Bible school was started that was to grow until eventually graduates would become pastors of small churches throughout the tribe. Mary McIlrath (Catto) also was to have a valuable ministry in this school during its formative days.

Since its value to the future work was recognized, the school was carefully nurtured from its inception. But there were many problems connected with the school. Besides that of discipline and the supplying of the students' daily ration of sweet potatoes, there was the matter of orienting teenagers to study. Most of the students came to the Bible school illiterate. Fortunately, the Kapauku young people had developed in their growing-up years the faculty for remembering things that they had learned or heard. Much effort was invested in making the first students in our Bible School literate as quickly as possible. Marion Doble was to contribute valuable aid and techniques in achieving this end.

After a few weeks of training, the students were sent out on weekends to witness for Christ. They would scatter in various directions after classes were over on Friday. It was a thrill to see the canoes radiating out over the lake from Enarotali. They had been drilled in the gospel story that they were to relate. Sometimes they were not so good at remembering important details of the story they were giving out. Nevertheless, over the months and years, definite progress and improvement was noticed. On Sunday afternoons, these students would return to Enarotali and on Monday morning report the reactions to their ministry.[2]

Although teaching had been my dream, and standing in front of a class of Bible school students made me feel like a fish *in* water, I also knew myself to be singularly unprepared for this task. The only textbook available was the Kapauku New Testament translated by Marion Doble. My notes from the theology classes that I had preserved from my days in the Brussels Bible Institute needed more than being translated into the vernacular; they had to be completely reworked, sometimes even reinvented.

The students, who were still only barely literate, were very good at memorizing but poor in independent thinking or applying biblical truths to practical situations. As a result, they demanded to be given questions with corresponding answers to study. These were committed to memory in an unquestioning fashion. They were not only quite upset if I made little changes in the questions when giving exams, but were completely thrown off when I changed the numbering of the questions. After all, they had studied the questions and answers in their correct sequence. So, if for instance, I marked a random question as number three on the blackboard, I would receive the answer number three from the book, regardless of the contents of the question. This made me decide to introduce true-and-false questions, thus forcing their gray cells to kick in.

Teaching the young people was a challenge. It was a challenge I loved. I particularly appreciated the fact that I could concentrate on only one thing—teaching Bible school—and I did not have to wear three or four different hats.

Our year in Enarotali was disturbed by recurring attacks of amoebic dysentery. One of the worst came one day after the birth of our third child, Michel André, who made his entrance into this world on June 30, 1961. He was a beautiful baby.

While Janine was still recuperating, the lab report from the local hospital came with the word that the problems I had experienced were due to an acute attack of amoebic dysentery. The doctor recommended that I be treated with shots of emitine, which required complete bed rest for about five days. Since Janine was still recuperating, five days of bed rest for me was out of the question; so I opted for pills of a milder form that would keep me ambulant.

Two days of pills, however, only drove the amoeba into my liver and caused excruciating and immobilizing pain. So, on the day Janine was able to get up, I went down. For the next several months, I was administered one amoebic treatment after another. My intermittent sickness was not conducive to a good and regular teaching schedule; I knew that the students suffered along with me. I did not begin to return to normal until we went on furlough.

Enarotali became a growing settlement. When Einar Mickelson had first started the Bible school, there was an abundance of land that could be converted into sweet potato gardens. The construction of a small airfield and the increase of travel, as a result of this, promoted growth which made the availability of more gardens a problem. The increase of our student population also made us consider the possibility of moving elsewhere. Walter Post, who had been the director of the school before going on furlough, was consulted by mail. He agreed that we should consider relocation.

Together with Ken Troutman, who was the senior missionary on the station, I made several trips across the lake to look for suitable spots. The Mission owned land on the other side of the lake, in Obano, where a school had been located previous to the uprising in 1956. The location was good, and although the hostilities had died down, the attitude of the people was still far from friendly. Kebo, on the north shore of the lake, was quite different. The people invited us to locate the school in their area, and they also offered us a large piece of ground free of charge. So, by the end of our first term on the field, it was decided that the Kapauku Bible School would move to Kebo.

This was not the only change that would take place during our first furlough. The relationship between the Republic of Indonesia and the Netherlands had been very antagonistic. The point of contention was Dutch New Guinea. Before World War II, New Guinea had been part of the Dutch East Indies, and although the island had been treated more as a stepchild than a lucrative possession, it was never considered to be a separate colony. Sukarno, Indonesia's president was adamant: Dutch New Guinea, or West New Guinea, as he called it, was part of the Republic of Indonesia. A new name was invented for that part of the island: Irian Jaya. "Jaya" means "glorious," and "Irian" is supposed to be an acrostic for Initiative of the Republic of Indonesia Anti Netherlands. (This derivation is disputed by some.) The name stuck even after relations between the two countries became friendly several years later.

Sukarno launched a token war against the Dutch colonial government by dropping paratroopers over the island. The paratroopers were supposed to repossess the territory for Indonesia. Most of them were dropped off along the south coast and had to trek through the jungle west of Enarotali to the north coast. Many of them arrived there in a semi-starved condition and were picked up by the Dutch police and military. They were fed and pampered and returned to Indonesia in better condition than they had ever enjoyed. In spite of this implausible performance, Sukarno cleverly manipulated world opinion. Finally, under the auspices of the United Nations, the Bunker Plan was set in motion.

Conceived by a later American ambassador to Vietnam of the same name, Elsworth Bunker, the plan provided for a gradual transfer of West New Guinea from a Dutch administration to an Indonesian form of government. The stipulation was that Indonesia would rule the island for a trial period of five years, after which a plebiscite would be held. At that time, the Papuan population could decide whether they wanted to be part of Indonesia or become an independent country like the eastern part of the island, either separately or together as one state. More about this in a later chapter.

When we left for our first furlough in late 1961, none of this had been made public. Sukarno was still dropping his parachutes over Dutch New Guinea. I must confess that we felt somewhat relieved to be able to leave a tense situation behind us.

Going home on a first furlough was almost as dramatic an experience as going to the mission field for the first time. In later years, we got used to switching back and forth to the point where going home felt like never having been away and going back to the mission field felt like never having left.

Our first furlough, the great part of which we spent at the home of Janine's parents in Belgium, was a time of testing. I came down with my first attack of malaria two weeks after our arrival. Not suspecting I had contracted the sickness, I thought the Lord was calling me home prematurely which, to my amazement, was an exhilarating experience. Then followed a prolonged spell of hepatitis which I must have picked up in New Guinea just prior to our departure. But the worst was the news that broke upon us in July of that year. The government of Dutch New Guinea was going to be transferred from the Netherlands to Indonesia. That made our return at the end of the year's furlough very unlikely. Strangely and suddenly, we both realized how much we loved the people and the place to which the Lord had called us.

The Dutch Alliance Committee, which was responsible to raise the money for our return, was very pessimistic about our prospects due to the political uncertainty after the Indonesian takeover. They were not willing to raise the funds. In the meantime, the Alliance in the United States had invited us to come to Nyack to see how the society, under whose auspices we had been sent out, worked in the homeland. At Nyack, I audited some classes at the college and visited the national headquarters in New York City and churches in the area.

Meanwhile, we also needed a new visa to be able to return to the field. The business manager of the Alliance took me to the headquarters of the United Nations, which at that time had temporary control of what had been Dutch New Guinea. They saw no problem in our return, and the visas were stamped in our passports without further ado. This stimulated the Dutch office to raise money for our return trip. A fund-raising ad was placed in *De Pionier,* the Dutch Mission's magazine. One person, unknown to us, was about to deposit $2,500 in his bank account when he read the ad. He changed his mind and sent the whole amount to the Mission. If we had had any doubt about our return, the Lord surely dispelled it in an efficient way!

We returned to Irian Jaya with great expectations; however, we were rather apprehensive as to what we would find on the political scene. The Dutch presence in West New Guinea, as it was now called, diminished rapidly and Indonesians filled their places in the government offices in Enarotali—two or three Indonesian officials for every Dutchman who left.

During our furlough, Walter and Viola Post had begun to move the Kapauku Bible School from Enarotali to Kebo. But moving the location was not the only change that was deemed necessary. In view of the new political scene, it was necessary to switch the school's curriculum from the vernacular to Indonesian, the official language of the Republic of Indonesia. Making Indonesian the language of the Bible school would open up the school for other tribes where Indonesian had already become a second language for young people who were eager to be educated.

The first thing Walter Post had undertaken in Kebo was the construction of a small airfield where the single-engine planes of MAF could land. Flying back from our furlough assignment, we requested to be allowed to stop in Kebo to see progress on the development of the campus and to see the house in which we were going to live. We landed in Kebo and were met by Walter and Viola in addition to several students from the school. Also, Frans Titahelew, an Ambonese schoolteacher, who was skilled in carpentry work, was present. Frans had volunteered to oversee the construction of the buildings.

As we walked up the trail that led from the airstrip to the top of the hill where the Posts' residence had already been built, I asked Walter, "Where is our house?" He laughed rather sheepishly and, pointing to a heap of stones, answered: "It will be there." Moving to Kebo obviously would not take place in the next few days! In the meantime, we would need a place for our family, now consisting of Janine, Ruthy (four-and-a-half), John Paul (three), Michel (one-and-a-half) and me. A fourth child was about to make her appearance and, for that reason alone, it would be good for Janine to be in Enarotali in the vicinity of a hospital. So we moved to Enarotali and settled temporarily in the small house that had been our first residence when we had arrived as newlyweds five years before.

Ruthy was growing up fast. She could hardly wait to leave us to go to the school for missionaries' children in Sentani, 400 miles away from our jungle station. I explained to her that she would have to wait about one-and-a-half more years, which of course to her could be tomorrow morning.

"First," I said, "Mommy will have a baby, and then you will have a little more growing up to do." This last part was lost on her, as we found out later.

About six weeks after our arrival, Janine woke me up in the wee hours of the morning, saying that she thought the time had come. I walked the five yards that separated our house from the house where the Troutmans lived and woke up Vida. Her expert eye scanned Janine, and she expressed the opinion that maybe things were not quite normal. I immediately decided to go after medical help. By now, the Dutch doctors had disappeared, and an Indonesian physician of Chinese descent, Dr. Ong, a very pleasant person but not a seasoned medical officer, manned the local hospital. I went, therefore, not to the hospital but to the Catholic Mission where one of the nuns was a certified midwife.

As I made my way in the dark with the help of my flashlight to the small convent, I prayed that the Lord would not allow anything to go wrong with Janine and the baby. An almost audible voice said to me, "Fear not!" It was not an out-of-the-world experience, but a deep peace that descended upon me. In that moment, my anxiety ebbed away.

It was not difficult to wake Sister Bernardina since it was probably about the time for her morning prayers. After checking things out, she assured me that, at this point, there was no reason to fear, but she urged me to take Janine to the hospital as soon as it became light. Dr. Ong had already announced that he would not do any deliveries at home as the Dutch doctors had done before. This did not shake our confidence in Dr. Ong, but when I found him a few hours later sitting at the side of Janine's bed, her contractions coming rapidly and strongly, with a medical book on his lap and turning the pages as Janine's labor progressed, we realized that Janine must have been his first case! He was less prepared for this than we were! Praise the Lord for the presence of Sister Bernardina who very tactfully kept herself in the background, but who saw to it that Viviane, this beautiful fourth child of ours, came into this world smoothly and safely.

When I finally went uphill to announce the good news to the Troutmans, Vida said that Ruthy needed a word of parental counseling. When she woke up, Vida had told her that her mother was in the hospital having a baby. Ruthy's reaction was: "Then I am going to school." She went straight to the suitcase where her school clothing had been packed away, outfits we had brought back from the States for the years to come, and dressed herself in a dress twice her size. None of Vida's arguments had any effect. Her daddy had clearly explained to her the sequence of things to come: first the baby, then the school. There was some disappointment when I told her that she had overlooked some intermediate waiting periods. She finally settled for a smaller sized dress.

Several problems faced us: 1) it would be impossible for the family to move to Kebo until there was a place for us to live; 2) it would take several months before the house, erected according to Mission specifications, would be finished; 3) it would be necessary for me to spend most of my time in Kebo to see that a house was built. However, being away for most of the week and letting Janine fend for herself with the four children for the next several months was not desirable either. So I prevailed upon our good friend Frans Titahelew first to build the storage place that would be part of the house, and then to start the framework of the house to the point where the aluminum roof could be put on. This would take only a few weeks. Frans worked overtime and, as soon as the roof was on, we put a lining in the bathroom downstairs and in one of the bedrooms upstairs even before any outside walls were put up. With this temporary shelter in place, the family was called to move to Kebo.

How Janine managed to survive with four children in the storage shed and even run a household as if this was the most normal of all living conditions, I do not know, but I respected her even more deeply for it. She confirmed my convictions that the Lord had known all the time whom He had called for life in the jungle. Janine was made of the right fiber.

The storage shed was divided into three sections, living quarters of approximately ten by fifteen feet, a kitchen of ten by eight feet and a laundry shed of ten by ten feet. To say that our living quarters were crowded would be an understatement. When Janine did the cooking, there was no place for anybody else in the kitchen. We lost our wedding Bible when a whole pitcher of milk spilled and soaked the pages.

But the upstairs bedroom that housed every bed that we possessed was even more of a spectacle. Everybody had to climb over everybody else to crawl into his or her assigned niche. The advantage was that falling out of bed was not an option—there was no floor space left on which to fall! I can still see our little caravan going upstairs at night. Janine with a kerosene pressure lamp up front, the children climbing up the temporary stairway to the first floor in a house that had no walls and me bringing up the rear. It must have been quite a spectacle for anyone watching.

While Frans worked on the house, I wrestled with the construction of a 500-gallon water storage tank to catch the rainwater off the aluminum roof and feed it into the kitchen, shower and toilet. The tank had been ordered in Australia. It arrived in sections that had to be bolted together, then soldered.

The bolting part was easy, but I had never soldered before, and there were no ten-easy-soldering lessons available in the heart of the jungle. I secured a blowtorch, some sticks of solder and acid which I had to combine in the right proportions at the right tempera-

WAR—AND THE JUNGLE ADVENTURE 61

ture. Just when the finished product was hoisted on a stand, high enough for gravity to feed the water into the house, the rains stopped. I could only hope that I had done a good job. Walter Post good-naturedly poked fun at me by spreading the word that my drum was not leaking, mainly because of lack of rain!

When the rains did come, and my work was tested, it turned out that I had to do the job all over again, this time adding tar and strips of cloth to the seams. When all the work was finally finished, we had a rather sophisticated setup by which the water caught from the roof would run through the firebox of the woodstove via copper tubing and provide the kitchen and the shower with hot water twenty-four hours a day.

The experiment would have given me more pleasure if I had not suffered from recurring bouts of tonsillitis which put me to bed with a high fever about once a month. Finally, Janine procured penicillin which she would shoot into me with great agility so I could go back to work.

After about five months, the house was completed, and we now began thinking of the ministry we had come to do. I would now be teaching in Indonesian, a language I had never officially studied. Coming over on the boat, I had worked through a small book I had bought in Holland, called *Bahasa Indonesia*, the language which helped me to carry on simple conversations with the Indonesian-speaking schoolteachers. Such conversation was a far cry from teaching Bible in Indonesian.

A complicating factor was that the Indonesian Bible was a combination of two translations, made by foreign missionaries working in the Dutch East Indies. The Old Testament translation was about 100 years old, and the New Testament had been finished just before the outbreak of World War II. Compared to modern Indonesian, this was an archaic language. A small consolation was that the students, for all of whom Indonesian was a foreign language, knew even less than I did. So I accepted the challenge. I found out that there are two good ways to learn a language: 1) marry a girl who speaks it, which was the way I improved my French, and 2) teach the language to someone else.

Janine showed great ability in picking up Indonesian, and it did not take long till she was able to start a fruitful ministry among the women of the school, most of whom were wives of students. So we embarked upon a thirteen-year-long adventure in Kebo, teaching in the Kebo Bible School, and spending the most wonderful years of our lives in the heart of the jungle.

Endnotes

1. Before World War II, some Christians from other Indonesian islands accompanied the first missionaries into Dutch New Guinea. Paksoal and Ladjang were Christians from the Moluccas.

2. E.H. Mickelson, *God Can.* (N.P., 1966), p. 159.

5

The People Who Heal People

Finally the time arrived for Ruthy to go to school. In order to soften the trauma for all of us, we took a vacation as a family and went to Sukarnapura (later called Jayapura). It was located about twenty-five miles from Sentani, where the MK school was located.

It was hard to leave our six-year-old daughter behind and go back to our jungle station. We found that we would never get used to the separation which only got worse as our children left home one by one in the next six years. Invariably, after the little MAF plane took off with our precious load, Janine and I would walk back to the house, which was only a few hundred yards from the airstrip, but which seemed a miles' long trek through barren land. We would go upstairs, sit on the edge of our bed and cry together. Then we would pray, and every time the miracle was faithfully repeated—the Lord took the burden of sadness off our shoulders and allowed us to go back to work with peace of mind.

Janine and I considered that sending our children away to boarding school was the only real sacrifice we ever made for the Lord. Everything else was easy in comparison. The lack of comfort and civilization never disheartened us, and we learned to relax without the help of TV or other distractions that are part of Western culture. But seeing our children leave us left an inexpressible void which God somehow filled every time. He faithfully wiped every tear from our eyes. Their prolonged absence during the school year also made their time at home more precious. Every year we spent at least four months of quality time with our children at home. It made us grow into a closely knit family with a deep love for each other.

Years later, Ruthy wrote an article for the Dutch Magazine *De Pionier*, which I copy here:

> In many respects it is a privilege to be a Missionary Kid. It is a pleasant life in which you have experiences no other kid has.
>
> I am at present a seventeen-year-old M.K., and this is, of course, the only life I know. After I was born, my parents moved from Enarotali to Tigi, and later back to Enarotali. After our first furlough, we moved to Kebo, where my parents are now still working as teachers at a Bible school. It will be hard for me to leave Irian Jaya after seventeen years. I am dreaming to be able to come back here and do missionary work myself, but I don't

know what plans the Lord has for me. I love the people here, and I would like to continue the work my parents are doing.

To be an M.K. is one of the finest things in the world. You not only see the work your parents are doing, but you also see other cultures, and you have the opportunity to do a lot of traveling. We are more privileged than most children in Europe or America.

People often pity children of missionaries, but I don't find this is necessary. Although we do not see our parents eight months out of the year, we have a good family life. Because we are often away from home, we feel the family bond much closer. We long to be home when we are away at school, and when we do go home, we really enjoy being together.

We see God at work in a wonderful way in this part of the world. The less civilized people, who have never had a chance to hear the gospel, are now turning to the Lord and away from their spirit worship. Within our families also, we see God working with healing and other kinds of miracles.

I wouldn't want to trade this kind of life for anything in the world. I love it.

When we struggled with the idea of letting our children go, the Lord graciously reminded us of a promise we had made. Before the children were born, we had dedicated them to the Lord. We renewed our promise when they were born. We even asked Him not to give us any children who wouldn't follow Him. We could send our children away with the assurance that the Lord would take care of them. This brought great comfort to our hearts.

As we worked ourselves into the routine of teaching and our grasp of the language improved, our medical ministry also grew rapidly. The hospital in Enarotali was no longer the medical center it had been during the time when the Dutch doctors ran the place. There were no more campaigns to eradicate the tropical diseases that plagued the tribal people. Some of them, like yaws, made a comeback, and previously unknown sicknesses entered the mountains. Measles, whooping cough and chicken pox began to claim victims, especially among the little children. Infant mortality was frightfully high.

I did a simple survey, asking the women of the village how many children they had borne. The answer would usually be between five and eight.

"How many are still alive?" I asked.

The answer often was one or two. Although death was considered a significant part of everyday life, most people showed little or no emotion when an infant died. This numbness was hard for us to accept.

The people observed that in our family of four children, none of them had died. In the eyes of the people this put us in a position of spiritual power that was beyond their reach. Mothers who brought their children to us realized that in most cases the child's sickness would be over in only a few days. Pneumonia and dysentery, the greatest killers among the mountain tribes, were easy to diagnose even for us who had no medical training, and the distribution of antibiotics performed many miracles. The disappearance of the ugly, painful sores of yaws after only one shot of oil-based penicillin was considered the greatest miracle. Our little clinic became famous, and we were honored with the appellation of "the people who heal people."

Every day we spent a considerable part of our time treating sick people, often squeezing care of the sick between two hours of teaching. This had not been part of our job description, and it was not even part of the official task description of The Christian and Missionary Alliance for the missionaries the Society sent out. In those years, medical ministries were a negligible part of the Alliance. It was only in later stages, as the Mission reached out to more primitive fields, that the message of divine healing was supplemented with medical ministries. We found it impossible to see the heartrending conditions of the sick around us and not be moved with compassion to give all the help we could possibly give. How could one give the gospel for the soul without giving help for the body?

In February of 1964, I wrote an article for *De Pionier*:

> We were awakened at an unusually early hour by a woman with a baby. It was still dark. Our first reaction was that the woman should be patient and wait till the usual time when we give out medicine. But when Janine opened the kitchen door and let her in, and

the woman took her child out of the carrying net, we changed our mind rapidly. It was clear that the poor creature had an advanced case of dysentery. His eyes were sunken, and from time to time they turned inward. The mother told us that she had wanted to come in the middle of the night, but no one wanted to come with her in the dark.

Most tribespeople are scared in the dark unless they carry a burning stick to shed light and to keep evil spirits away. Janine gave some medication to the little one and told the woman to come back in a few hours, but the mother could not be moved out of our kitchen.

About one hour later, a second mother came with a child with exactly the same symptoms. The baby had gotten sick three days before while the parents were away to visit family or carry on some other business. The dysentery became more and more serious. This child's condition was just as hopeless as the first one. We prayed that the Lord would have mercy on both of them. Janine went to look from time to time. She was just as anxious about those children as if they were her own.

Before noon the first child died. The mother had never left our kitchen. It dawned on the second mother how serious the condition of her child was. She kept saying to Janine: "He's still alive, he's still alive." When she came back the next morning, with the baby still alive, our hope rekindled, and we thought he would pull through. But the third day, a Sunday, the mother did not come, nor on the following Monday.

We haven't seen her since. We heard from other people that the second child had died also. The devil uses hopeless cases like that to attack God's servants.

Cases like these made us realize that the Lord wanted us to do more than just teach and preach the Word. The following excerpts from my 1968 diary provide a glimpse into the smorgasbord of activities that filled our days.

July 12, 1968: I worked in the school office this morning to prepare the lesson roster for the new semester. The students will not arrive until August 7.

July 13: Willem Patty, our Indonesian teacher, is sick. I visited him and gave him Tri-Sulfa. He said he felt better in the evening.

July 14: We had an Indonesian church service in our home. After that, I went to the service in the local tribal language in the village church. This was the first time I was able to go to that church after coming back from furlough. I was happily surprised to see over 600 people there.

July 15: Ruthy left by plane for Hitadipa. The Cutts family had invited her to come and spend a week with their daughter, Amy, before they had to go back to school. The plane came back for a group of Damal evangelists from the Beoga Valley, who had gone on foot to the Koyong area, and had been on the trail for two months. Willem Patty is very sick today. I gave him malaria pills.

July 16: Patty called me this afternoon because he thought he was going to die. He was ready to meet the Lord, but his wife wept bitterly. They have three small children. I didn't think that he was really dying. It looked as if his stomach could not take the strong malaria medicine. I tried to call the doctor via the transmitter radio, but the static was so bad that she couldn't understand what I said. This made me extremely anxious.

July 17: Patty called again about 12 midnight. He could not stop vomiting, so I gave him a motion sickness pill. In the morning I called the doctor who said I have to give Patty some sleeping pills. Bill Cutts called from Hitadipa to say that Ruthy was sick and running a high fever. I called the MAF base in Sentani by radio to ask for a plane to bring her home. One of their pilots made a special flight. Hitadipa is about twenty minutes flying time from Kebo. Patty is recovering.

July 27: When I tried to charge the radio battery, I broke the sediment bowl of the generator. I was able to patch it up with fiberglass. In the afternoon I worked in my darkroom for the first time since returning from furlough. I printed some pictures. After that I worked on a sermon for the Indonesian service on Sunday.

July 28: We had another Indonesian service in our home, and after that I went to the local village church where Theo Gobai preached. Theo is a Kapauku whom we sent to Makassar for further study. Two years ago, he was operated on for a brain tumor. Recently, he returned to Kebo to become the pastor of the village church. In the afternoon, I went to look at a cow that was supposed to be giving birth to a calf.

July 29: I went at least four or five times to look at the cow, because something is obviously wrong. I tried to contact the veterinary assistant in Enarotali by radio, but did not succeed.

July 30: The assistant crossed the lake by motorboat in heavy rain. His advice: "Don't do anything! The calf is probably premature, and this is an abortion. Everything will be OK." I felt reassured.

July 31: Paid the salaries of the workers (carpenter, airfield crew). After that I opened our little store so the workers would have a chance to spend their money. While I was very busy serving my customers and helping them to make up their minds, somebody entered the store to tell me that the cow had just died. That report precipitated the closing of the store as we hurried to the site of the tragedy. As a large and curious crowd gathered, the cow was skinned and quartered, and the meat was hung up till the next morning. I called the MAF in Nabire by radio to ask for a plane to Enarotali, where part of the meat can be sold tomorrow.

August 2: The mimeograph machine broke. I replaced the straps and ran off copies of my course on Romans. After prayer meeting at our house, one of our students arrived in very poor condition. He was running a high fever and had trouble breathing. He had rowed about eight miles in a native dugout canoe from his village to the school. I gave him a shot of penicillin. If he had waited until the next day, he would probably not have made it.

August 4: Two students came over the trail from Beoga, a trek of eleven days. The sick student is doing better.

August 5: The students from the Tigi district arrived. It was a hassle to show everyone his place. Several keys for padlocks on the doors were missing, and we had to cut off several locks with a hacksaw. Yunus Gobai, who is the district superintendent of the Kebo area, and also a member of the school board, came to receive tuition from the students and to pay the salaries of the national teachers. It took a very long time to find out why his accounts didn't balance and how much he had to pay each of the teachers. The abundant rainfall threatens our sweet potato crop. We have begun to pray that the Lord would stop the rain. It seems that the Lord is answering.

August 6: Elze Stringer, our fellow Dutch missionary, came today. She has to check the Preparatory Bible School in a village about one hour's walk from here. The boat came from Obano with students from the valleys west of the Wissel Lakes. Bill Cutts called by radio to say that the father of two of the students from his area had passed away suddenly. The boys cried when I told them. I prayed with them. "He was a rich man," they said, "but he was not a believer in Jesus." My heart went out to them. One of the boys wants to walk back to Hitadipa. This will take him about seven days on the trail. There is a danger that after the burial the people will want to kill one of the dead man's wives. The custom of the tribe is to send a wife along with a deceased chief to accompany him on the way to the kingdom of death.

August 7: School started.

6

Sometimes the Twain Do Meet

"What is your name?" I asked one of the younger boys in my class.

"I have no name," came the reply. I had heard about the phenomenon where people hesitate to pronounce their name for fear of evil spirits who pounce on people whose identity is known. For that reason, newborn babies sometimes remained nameless until the time came that they would need to have a name by which they could be called. At that point, names were given which would hide the child's identity rather than reveal it. A girl might be called "the girl without legs." No evil spirit would show any interest in such a person.

The boy I asked turned out to be Japebwi, "child of war." He was born during a tribal war, but he didn't tell me that, nor did any of his friends. I asked the other boys, "What is his name?"

"We are his friends. We cannot tell you that!" they retorted with some indignation. For that reason, as soon as people would hear the gospel and experience salvation, they would exchange their tribal name for a Christian one. Japebwi began to call himself Theophilus and later abbreviated it to Theo.

Two boys, Musa and Timotheus, wanted to see me about a marriage problem. What their original names were, I don't know. But I knew that the name Musa was the Indonesian version of Moses. After the boys seated themselves in my study, I soon discovered that marriage problems in Kapauku society are of a different nature than those in Western culture. I found it extremely difficult to follow what the boys were trying to communicate to me. The fact that Musa began his story in a rather roundabout way didn't help my understanding. It was about his "sister," at least that's what he called her. The woman may have been his aunt or cousin in the complicated system of family relations within the tribe, but the term "sister" covers many of them. So, his sister, when she was still a young girl, had married a man from another village down the valley. Musa's "brothers" (or uncles) had, at that time, received several strings of beautiful cowry shells as a bride price.

A few years later, the sister's husband died. Because her brothers-in-law did not feel inclined to further assist her, they asked for their shells back. The shells were returned, and the widow went back to her parental home.

After a while, a new candidate showed up who wanted to marry the girl. But since she was not young anymore (Kapauku women age fast), this man was not willing to put down too much of a bride price. Neither were the shells he offered first-class quality. However, since there was little chance of a better deal, the shells were accepted, and Musa's sister married for the second time. But at the transfer of the bride price, it turned out that fifty shells were missing. There was some protest, but finally the matter was dropped. Timotheus was born into this second marriage. That made Musa and Timotheus "cousins" and apparently good friends also. They were approximately the same age. Musa told me that he had never looked angrily at Timotheus because of those fifty missing shells. Actually, Musa had forgiven his cousin!

As I listened to the story, I had to force myself to remember that neither Musa nor Timotheus was born when this bride price was paid. But now the time had come for Timotheus to get married. The main factor, or at least the most important one in any kind of marriage contract in Kapauku culture, seems to be the bride price, consisting of cowry shells, some of which are antique and have circulated in the tribe for generations. Musa was so magnanimous that he was willing to help Timotheus with the bride price he had to pay. This, I found out, was in fact Timotheus' plan.

At this point, the plot thickened.

Timotheus' sister was also about to be married off, and the shells Timotheus would receive from that deal would help him to seal his own marriage contract. (Are you still with me?) The day of the sister's wedding, when the shells were transferred, Musa went along with Timotheus. When Musa saw how beautiful the shells were that Timotheus was about to receive, he suddenly forgot his magnanimity and remembered those fifty shells that had been missing when Timotheus' mother got married. I say "remembered," but, of course, Musa was not born yet when the transactions took place. Conveniently forgetting the anachronism of the matter, Musa helped himself to fifty beautiful shells.

"Why don't you first pay me for your mother?" he asked Timotheus. But Timotheus didn't like the suggestion, and he became furious. This was the reason that the two had come to me. Solomon's wisdom was needed here!

In the meantime, Musa had somewhat changed his mind and declared himself to be ready to give the fifty shells back if he would receive three shells more precious and more beautiful in return. My sermon about covetousness and Christian witness had very little effect upon Musa. He seemed to feel that he ought to get at least something out of the deal.

At this point, Musa's "sister" (Timotheus' mother) joined the conversation. She listened to the quarrel, and the fact that the bride price of her own wedding was being discussed did not seem to hold any embarrassment for her. I never heard how the two cousins solved their dispute. It could very well be that they never did and that their children or grandchildren will bring up the matter and fight about it for decades to come. I began to wonder if I would ever be able to cross the bridge that separates the East from the West. Maybe Kipling was right: "Never the twain shall meet."

It seemed that the main reason most of our students came to the Kebo Bible School was that it had a reputation of good quality and it was a place to receive an education. A desire to become a well-trained servant of the Lord was not always their principal motivation. To become proficient in Indonesian and even to learn some English were often overriding concerns for many. We were not even convinced that all of our students were Christians. But the fact that they were daily exposed to the preaching of the gospel during the chapel services and had to apply themselves to a systematic study of the Bible proved to have a lasting effect.

Many who came out of curiosity or with mixed motives found the Lord during their four years of study. The fact that the faculty spent every morning between 11 and 12 in prayer for the students and the needs of the school eventually opened the door for the Holy Spirit to do His work. Walter Post had initiated this daily prayer meeting, and, after the Posts left the field, I continued this practice with the Indonesian and indigenous staff members.

The Lord also had other means at His disposal to get the students' attention: hunger. The staple food for the mountain tribespeople of Irian Jaya is the sweet potato. There is something of everything the body needs in the sweet potato, and although it doesn't make for an appetizing diet, it is possible for man to live on sweet potatoes alone. The Kebo Bible School possessed a rather large property, most of which was at the students' disposal for use as gardens. The policy was that the students who came to school were given a garden with a certain number of prepared beds of sweet potatoes, according to the size of their families. They would keep themselves supplied with sweet potatoes by maintaining their own gardens.

At graduation they would leave behind the same number of prepared beds they had received when they first arrived. This system generally worked well. But one year Irian Jaya's abundant rainfall outdid itself. There were weeks of uninterrupted rain. The gardens flooded several times, and the sweet potatoes began to rot before they could be harvested.

The students knew that their food supply was dwindling, but they did not tell me how critical the situation was. One of the biblical principles they strictly adhere to is never to worry about tomorrow. So they waited till the bitter end came.

One afternoon, about 4 o'clock, the president of the student council came to inform me that all the potatoes were gone and that the students had had nothing to eat since "yesterday morning." I reacted to this information in a very unspiritual way: I blew my top! I told the council president that I felt that fasting would enhance their prayer life. This was not very sensitive of me to give that piece of advice. As I walked home and went into my study, I felt like Moses must have felt carrying the burden of the people of Israel. What was I going to do to solve this problem?

I realized that our Father in heaven "sends rain on the righteous and the unrighteous," and that the people in the surrounding villages had had the same amount of rain on their gardens as the students in our Bible School had on theirs. The chance that we would be able to buy sweet potatoes from people in the villages was very slim. Yet, seeing no other way out, my mind went in that direction. If only the rain would stop!

To say that our mountain tribespeople are scantily dressed would be an understatement. When it rains early in the morning, they hate to go out into the cold mountain air to their gardens even to dig potatoes for themselves, let alone for someone else. So my first and only prayer was: "Lord, please, stop the rain, and give us a nice sunny morning tomorrow!"

When I awoke the next morning, the first thing I did was to look outside. There was not a healthy downpour, but one of those miserable drizzles that chills one to the bone. I threw up my hands and laughed. It was a strange reaction, but I felt that the devil had overstepped his boundaries by a few feet. There was nothing I could do now, so I turned the matter over to the Lord. Then, as I went down to the kitchen to start the woodstove and make some coffee, I heard someone knocking on the door. There stood a man from the village.

"I understand you need sweet potatoes," he said after we greeted each other. I couldn't have agreed with him more.

"I am building a house with nails, and I have run out of nails," he continued.

I knew what he was saying. Progress for these people meant moving away from their hut made with split boards planted in the ground, with a fireplace in the middle, and a bark roof on top, and building a house like the missionary's, with nails, a tin roof, a bed and blankets. I also realized that this man, just like our students, had not planned ahead. I thought it well not to mention this.

"If you can give me five pounds of nails, I'll give you a burlap bag full of sweet potatoes," he said. We signed the contract right then and there. And before breakfast time, there was a meal for the whole student body.

The churches in the surrounding villages and outlying areas heard that the students were hungry, and they began to take up offerings, not of money, but of sweet potatoes. They brought them in, sometimes only enough for one meal, sometimes enough for several days. At one point we had a supply enough for two weeks. The Lord kept us provided with His "manna" till vacation time. The Holy Spirit taught our students a lesson that I could not have given them in a classroom setting. They learned the truth of God's promise in the Psalms: "Call upon me in the day of trouble; I will deliver you, and you will honor me" (Psalm 50:15). It left a lasting impression upon their souls.

The real breakthrough came a few years later when we were on furlough in Europe. It was 1967. A revival had swept the Indonesian island of Timor. One of the principal means of God's grace was a man by the name of Mel Tari. Mel's brother-in-law, Frans Selan, came to Irian Jaya and was invited to hold meetings for the students at the Kebo Bible School. In his simple messages, Frans told the students that they had to get rid of all their fetishes and good luck charms. To the amazement of the missionary who had taken our place that year, the students turned out to be loaded with charms. It had never dawned on us, with our Western approach to evangelism, that converts to Christianity would keep charms that linked them to their former religious practices.

The new believers, however, thought that the only thing that had to be given up at conversion was black magic. They also decided that the corresponding fetishes should be discarded, but they saw no point in getting rid of good luck charms or fetishes that would stimulate the harvest of their gardens, ensure the health of their pigs or make a girl fall in love with a boy or vice versa. When they were told that both black magic and white magic came from the same source, the devil, they were amazed, convicted and repentant. A whole pile of charms was collected in front of the school building and burned.

The sparks jumped over to their souls. The students went out to witness to the villages around the Wissel Lakes. Churches mushroomed, and new churches were born overnight. The revival meetings in the Kebo Bible School changed the spiritual climate of the whole area.

When we returned from furlough, we found that the oppression had lifted, and the Holy Spirit was working freely. I still have reservations about some things that happened during the revival in Timor itself. That miracles happened is beyond doubt, but some of the things reported may not have been as supernatural as they sounded and can be explained by the Asian world philosophy and their approach to reality. But that the Holy Spirit was at work during the meetings at Kebo Bible School is an undeniable fact.

Our personal contacts with leading people in the villages close to the Bible school changed. One of the village chiefs, an intelligent though uneducated fellow by the name of Naiditaka, often came to visit, usually in order to obtain some goodies. Once, he asked for some passion fruit, the delicious purple egg-like fruit that grew on a vine on the garden fence. I gave him some and said: "These are only for your stomach. How about something for your soul?"

"I go to church sometimes," he replied, "and last Christmas I gave a pig to the church for their celebration."

"You think that will get you to heaven?" I asked. He wasn't sure, but he hoped so. We talked some more and went home. I didn't think he was convinced.

Later, he came back to ask questions about the "Jesus Word," as they called the Scriptures. He obviously understood the implications of a surrender of his life to the Lord because he said: "If someone comes to my hut, armed with his bow and arrows, and he starts an argument with me, I go into my hut and get my own weapons to defend myself. If I give my life to Jesus, I won't be able to do that anymore. I cannot counter evil with evil." I was amazed at his perceptivity, and I prayed that he would come to the point of opening the door of his heart to God. Sometime later, he did just that and asked to be baptized in the local river that flows along our campus.

Another frequent visitor was Pidopi, a man with only one eye who used to be the local witch doctor. He would sit in our living room and ask for a cup of tea which he called "the white man's water." We served him tea and gave him a box of matches which he preferred over his native fire maker. Lighting a fire in the jungle of Irian Jaya at one time was a major achievement. A man would put a stick of fresh wood under his two feet on top of some dry moss or leaves and rapidly move back and forth a piece of jungle vine around the stick. The friction would cause enough heat to start a smoldering smoky fire in the moss. A much easier life had come for those Stone-Age people when they learned to strike a match along the side of a little box. Pidopi was never very much interested in spiritual things; however, he assured me that he had never stolen anything, never committed adultery and never told a lie.

One day, Pidopi's son came to tell us that his father was sick with dysentery. We gave some medication to the boy and told him to come back after a few days. He came back later to tell us that the medicine had not helped. *If dysentery doesn't respond to the strong antibiotics we gave him, then something else must be the matter,* I thought. I decided to pay a visit to Pidopi's house. I found him very sick, at the point of death.

"My friend, you are going to die," I told him. "Where do you think you will go?" He gave me the same line that he had boasted before about his impeccable behavior.

I countered with, "But you have been a witch doctor. You talked to spirits and cast spells on people. Jesus hates that." This shocked him.

He admitted his previous contacts with the occult and cried, "I don't want to go into the fire." Thinking of Paul's words, "Everyone who calls on the name of the Lord will be saved," I urged him to simply call on the Lord Jesus.

"Jesus, help me!" he prayed.

That was all. It was enough. I went home, and later that afternoon I sloshed through the same mud to make another visit to Pidopi's hut. When I arrived, he had just died. I have no doubt that I will find Pidopi in the presence of the Lord when I get to heaven. But Pidopi's friends and family members thought differently. They could not believe that it was so easy. I too thought that it was almost too good to be true. But that's what God's Word says.

As often happens, this breath of fresh air, this spiritual spring time, was the forerunner of a brooding storm. A counterattack was on its way.

7

Rough but Precious Jewels

(written by Janine)

A missionary wife seems to have many challenges, among them adapting to a different culture, guarding her family's health, being a helpmate to her husband and carrying on a full-time ministry to the people. One of my greatest challenges, though, was learning to love the people.

The welcome we received from the tribal people when we first arrived was overwhelming. They received us with open arms, but I found it hard to reciprocate. All I could see were hundreds of primitive people jumping around with bows and arrows. I still remember, as I was coming out of the little plane upon our arrival, an old lady met me. She was wearing only a grass skirt, was very dirty and had a runny nose. She came up to me and gave me a big hug. She was so happy to welcome a new missionary wife! But

I wasn't happy! I was ready to jump back on the plane and go home. It is one thing to see pictures of such people, but a different thing to see them close up and in person.

"Are you sure you did not make a mistake in sending me to this primitive place?" I asked the Lord. "I'm not really prepared to work with these people. I will never fit." The Lord was very kind and patient and did not rebuke me. Instead, in a loving way, He reminded me of the promise I had made while in Bible school in Brussels, Belgium: "Lord, I will go wherever You want me to go." And here I was in the country of His calling, Irian Jaya. The Lord had called me to minister to these people to tell them about His love. How could I tell them about His love if I myself did not have love in my heart for them?

I prayed: "Lord, if You want me to minister effectively among these people, I ask You to do two things for me. First, help me to see them through Your eyes, people You have created, people who need to be saved, people for whom You died. Secondly, put Your love in my heart for them."

A miracle happened! The people did not change, but my feelings for them did. The fact that they were not clean and well dressed was not important anymore. I started to love them with the love of the Lord Jesus. This experience was very humbling for me, the missionary. Over the years, they became dear brothers and sisters in the Lord. Leaving them to come home to retire, I found out many years later, would be a heart-wrenching experience.

After language study, I was very uncertain as to what my ministry would be. I seemed to be so ill-equipped to do the work that was expected of me. I asked the Lord to open a door of ministry suited to my gifts. The Lord answered and allowed me to have a ministry among the women in the Bible school as well as in the village. In spite of the difference in backgrounds, culture and color, I made many good friends. One of them was Adriana Yeimo.

Adriana would never win a prize in a beauty contest. She is not a woman with polished manners; she can at times be rough in her speech. But because of her engaging smile and warm personality, I felt drawn to her. The stone-age culture of which she was a product accounts for her apparent roughness.

She grew up in Kegata, a small village nestled in the heart of high mountains and still untouched by western civilization. Life in the village was quite rugged for Adriana. At an early age, she had to learn to fend for herself. Her parents expected her to take a share in the daily work, planting gardens and raising pigs. Every morning she left the comfort of her warm hut to walk to the family gardens. The little grass skirt that was the only garment she was wearing didn't give her much protection against the morning chill. In an effort to stay warm, she would wrap her arms around her body and run to the gardens. There she put herself to the task of pulling out weeds from the sweet potato beds. Pretty soon, she felt the pangs of hunger and decided to dig some sweet potatoes to roast in a small wood fire. By this time, she felt pretty tired and would lie down to enjoy the warm sun.

Life would have gone on the same way if it hadn't been for a visiting team of evangelists bringing the gospel to remote villages. This good news revolutionized Adriana's life. It did not take her long to grasp the truth, and she opened her heart to the Lord. She felt a great hunger to learn more about this Jesus who had died on the cross in her place. The evangelists had left some portions of the gospels, but Adriana was illiterate.

In this primitive Stone-Age society, it wasn't fashionable for a girl to attend school. But she finally succeeded in convincing her parents to let her attend a literacy class taught by the local pastor. She proved to have a very keen mind, so it did not take her long to grasp the concept of reading. It was with great pride that a few weeks later she brought home a Bible lesson that she was able to read to her parents.

Soon the time arrived for Adriana to get married. One day she met Ben Yeimo. It is doubtful that it was love at first sight, as parents usually arrange marriages. The couple were united in marriage and promised to be faithful to each other both in good and bad times. Ben had found a capable wife, a virtuous woman, who was worth more than jewels to him. Adriana kept her promise to Ben to be a good and faithful wife. Together they dedicated their lives for the Lord's service. In this too she was faithful. Unfortunately, the same cannot be said about Ben.

In 1959, the Mission decided that in order to build a strong national church, the people should provide support for their own pastors. This was explained to the pastors during a conference, but it was not very well received. They all decided to go on strike and leave the ministry. Ben was among the dissenters. However, within twenty-four hours, everyone had come back except Ben. He took a government job.

Adriana was very hurt, but she decided in her heart to do her utmost to bring her husband back into the ministry. Through her prayers, wise counseling and loving concern, Ben was drawn again into the Lord's work. They both became teachers in the Kebo Bible School, and for several years we enjoyed working with them.

Adriana's heart was broken when Ben once again decided to leave the ministry to take a government job. They moved out of the highlands to the coastal area. While living there, Ben moved farther and farther away from the Lord. To this day he has not repented, but Adriana has faithfully stood by him, showing him love and patience.

During the years since I first met Adriana, in spite of her rough appearance, I felt drawn to her by her engaging smile, warm personality and keen sense of humor. We have spent many hours together, laughing about mistakes I made in her language and comparing stories about our children's antics. We also have cried together during times of hardship and sorrow, particularly when she lost one of her sons to dysentery. I also had the privilege of working with her in the Bible school in Kebo.

I praise the Lord for allowing me to share in the life of this godly woman, truly one of the Lord's precious jewels.

Many of our students were married and brought their wives with them to school. Since families arranged most of the marriages, the man had little to say in the choice of a wife. Several of the women students were illiterate and did not yet know the Lord. I felt a real burden to help them, not only academically, but also spiritually. Someday they would become pastors' wives, and I realized it would be disastrous if they didn't have a personal relationship with Jesus Christ. Therefore, I put all my efforts into teaching them to become women of God and helpers to their husbands.

Many had come from harsh backgrounds, their past obvious from the hardness on their faces. Teaching them was a challenge and at times frustrating when I saw little response. Many prayers went up to heaven to ask the Lord for a breakthrough in their lives. The Lord answered our prayers in a most wonderful way.

During some revival meetings at the school, many of the students rededicated their lives to the Lord and threw away the fetishes that were still bonding them to the devil. As I watched them go forward to get rid of all these things, I was amazed and puzzled that none of the women were following their husbands' examples. I knew that many of them were not really following the Lord.

The following day, I went to class. "Did you see what happened last night when your husbands went forward to get rid of their fetishes?" I asked.

No answer!

In simple Indonesian, I again explained the plan of salvation and the importance to free oneself from anything that keeps us away from the Lord.

No reaction!

I went home and asked our missionary colleagues to pray for the women that the Lord would open their eyes. The next day, I again explained what they should do to follow the Lord fully.

Again, no response!

Finally, on the third day, I detected a glimmer of hope. With tears streaming down their faces, they confessed that they had sinned against the Lord and had trusted the devil for their protection. They reached for their net bags and took out all kinds of objects—shells, stones, animals' tails, etc.—which they had kept to protect them and their families against attacks from the devil. They were now free women, and the Lord began to truly transform them from hard women to God-fearing women. What a joy it became to teach them from the Word of God and to see their eagerness to learn how to become virtuous women.

They have truly become precious jewels.

My main work after we moved to Nabire was to teach in the theological school; I still felt a burden to teach women. Mrs. Sumilat, the wife of the director of the school, and I started Bible studies for the students' wives and women from the village. Through the teaching of the Word of God, many lives were transformed. One example was Mrs. Yosina.

She became a Christian while attending the church services we had started for the students and people from the neighborhood. Her husband, a top man in the local government, was unfaithful to her and made life miserable for her and their two children. The government decided to send him to Jakarta, the capital, for further studies. She became very fearful at the thought that her husband would be away from her for several years. After all, if he was not faithful at home, what would happen when he was so far away? She found what she thought was a wonderful solution. She went to a local witch doctor in town with a request for help.

"Could you give me something that would assure me that my husband will stay faithful to me while he's away?" she begged.

The witch doctor answered, "No problem, I have just the right thing for this kind of problem. Here is this powder. Put it in his tea the morning he is due to leave for Jakarta, and I can assure you that this will work."

Mrs. Yosina paid her fee, took the powder and went home. The following morning, just before taking her husband to the airport, she made him a cup of tea and put the powder in it. With a light heart she said her good-byes. She had followed the witch doctor's instructions, and she knew her husband would be fine.

The following Wednesday, she came to our Bible study and told us about her husband's departure. She asked us to pray for him. We all prayed, asking the Lord to protect him and to keep him away from temptation. Of course, we were not aware of what Mrs. Yosina had done. The Lord knew, though, and would not give her any peace until she confessed her sin. That day, I spoke about things that could hinder our fellowship with the Lord. I stressed the importance of confessing sins to the Lord and asking for forgiveness.

Mrs. Yosina went home and started to think about what she had heard. In her heart and mind, she knew that things were not right between her and God. On Saturday, she attended our prayer cell and shared her problem.

"Why is it that when I pray, my prayer doesn't seem to reach the Lord? It feels like there is a wall between us. I try to read my Bible, but I don't get anywhere."

We prayed with her and asked the Lord to show her any sin that was still hidden in her heart.

A few days later, she came to us with tears in her eyes and confessed what she had done. She was doubtful that the Lord would ever forgive her for not trusting Him for her husband's faithfulness. We counseled with her and gave her the assurance that the Lord would forgive her if she would ask Him. She confessed her sin to the Lord and asked for His forgiveness, which, of course, He graciously gave her.

A few days later, with a gloomy look on her face, she came to our Wednesday Bible study. After the meeting she asked to talk to us. She explained that things were better between her and the Lord; however, something was still lacking. She wanted to know what the problem could be.

I was the missionary, an older woman. She expected an answer right then and there. Since I didn't have the gift of discernment, I asked the Lord to give me His wisdom so I would know what to say. God gave me an idea. I don't know why I hadn't thought of it myself!

"You have asked the Lord for forgiveness for what you have done to your husband, and He has forgiven you," I told her. "Now, I believe that if you want to be really free you should write your husband to confess what you have done and ask for his forgiveness."

"I can't do that!" she responded.

"Why not?" I asked.

"He will get angry."

"So what? He is thousands of miles away; he will not come to beat you up." She wasn't convinced that this was a good solution.

I prayed with her, asking the Lord to show her what she should do. The Lord showed her in a very clear way that, indeed, the right thing to do was to write to her husband. She did! Later, she came to our prayer meeting with a beaming face. Jokingly, I said to her: "You have done your homework, haven't you?"

With a big smile, she told us that she had written the letter and that she was feeling like a new person. She was now really free, and the Lord could start working in her life again. Sometime later she received news from her husband, but no mention of the letter. She felt quite relieved. Later, she told us that she had heard that her husband was living with another woman in Jakarta and had fathered a child. With a very sheepish look on her face, she confessed that the powder she had given her husband to keep him faithful had not worked. "I should have trusted the Lord, but I will keep praying for his salvation," she said. She believed that one day he would surrender his life to the Lord and serve Him.

The Lord wasn't through with Mrs. Yosina. He still had to do some cleaning up in her heart. During a ladies' retreat, the speaker stressed the importance of forgiving people, even those who had hurt us the most.

The Lord asked from her the ultimate—a complete surrender of her feelings toward a woman in town with whom her husband had had a relationship.

At the end of the meeting, the speaker gave an altar call for anyone who wanted to make things right with the Lord and with other people. Mrs. Yosina went forward!

Suddenly, I saw two women coming toward me. One sat on my left, the other on my right. I felt my heart skip a beat! "Lord, why are You doing this to me? Do You realize who those two women are?" I asked.

Of course He knew! One was Mrs. Yosina, the other her rival. They sat there for a while, nobody saying anything. Finally, I asked them to tell me what was on their minds.

"I cannot forgive her," said Mrs. Yosina. "She has wrecked my marriage and made life miserable for me and my two daughters."

The other lady, Mrs. M., admitted that she had been wrong and had sinned against the Lord and against Mrs. Yosina.

Turning toward her, she said, "What I have done to you is terrible, but I want to ask for your forgiveness. Please, would you forgive me?"

"There is no way I can forgive you," my friend answered bitterly. "What you are asking is too much."

In the meantime, I was praying that Mrs. Yosina would soften and find the grace to forgive.

Mrs. M. pleaded with her.

"The Lord has forgiven me. Why can't you forgive me also?"

Mrs. Yosina finally gave up, and with sincere tears told her rival that she was forgiven. What a victory! The three of us were crying, laughing and hugging each other. I know there was rejoicing in heaven because of this reconciliation.

A year or two later, Mrs. Yosina's husband, having finished his education, came back home. Because of his job, the whole family was transferred to Sentani. I did not see them again for several years. Then, during one of our visits in Sentani, I met her at the marketplace. We hugged each other and spent some time catching up on family news. She was beaming and shared some wonderful news with me. When her husband had come back home after his years of study, he saw a big change in his wife's attitude. She was no longer angry and bitter, but loving and supportive toward him. He was puzzled at the change in her and started to ask questions. This gave her an open door to explain what the Lord had done in her life. He was very impressed and started to seek the Lord himself. Some Christian brothers came to visit him and led him to receive Christ. My friend confessed that this would never have happened if she had not been obedient. She is truly the Lord's precious Irian Jaya jewel!

Ester was another rough jewel from one of the many islands of Indonesia. The Lord didn't have an easy time to refine her, but He never gave up. Very patiently and so lovingly, often through many difficult circumstances, He molded her and did a beautiful work in her life.

Ester was the wife of a military man who for many years had been stationed in Irian Jaya. Although she was uneducated and illiterate, she was intelligent and a very sharp businesswoman. I met her for the first time when we moved to the coastal town of Nabire. She faithfully attended our church services and ladies' meetings. I learned that she had gone through a lot of suffering in her life. She loved children, but was never able to have any herself. In that culture, barrenness is a great shame, and she was often the butt of cruel mocking.

Her husband was unfaithful to her and fathered several children by other women. At different times, he brought some of those children home for his wife to raise. Loving children as she did, she accepted the situation and poured her love on them. But not being loved by her husband was hard on her. She compensated for this by loving these little ones who loved her in return. In the meantime, she refused to have anything to do with her husband. They lived in the same house but didn't communicate at all. In her heart, she hated him for what he was doing to her, and she had lost all respect for him.

In one of our meetings, the Lord spoke to her in a very special way. I was teaching a lesson about the relationship of Christian women with their unbelieving husbands, that we should be loving, caring and patient. Just praying for them was not enough; we also had to show a Christlike example.

Ester went home, but she could not sleep that night. The Holy Spirit was starting to probe into her heart, and she was miserable. She knew that she had been a poor testimony and a bad example to her husband. She came to us and poured out her heart, telling us her life story. We knew about her husband's lifestyle, but we were not aware how bad it was. She wanted to know what she could do to repair this broken relationship.

"Lord," I prayed, "what do I tell this woman who has suffered so much at the hands of her husband? Please, give me Your wisdom to say the right words!"

"Go back home," I told her, "and do something special for him."

"What could I do for him?" she asked. "I haven't cooked for him in years. I have ignored him all this time. How can I get close to him again?"

"I have an idea," I said. "Go home, kill one of your chickens and cook him a nice meal. Put the food on the table with two plates and call him to eat. Then sit down with him and see what happens!"

She wasn't convinced that this was a good idea.

"He is going to think I am crazy," she said. I convinced her to try anyhow.

A few days later, she came to prayer meeting with a huge smile on her face.

"You did your homework, didn't you?" I asked, once again using my favorite expression.

"Yes," she said, "and it worked. I cooked a nice meal, put the food on the table and invited my husband to come and eat. He looked at me as if I had lost my mind.

"What's wrong with you, woman? You haven't cooked for me in years. What do you want from me?"

I told him just to sit down and eat, and we would talk. The hardest thing for me was to ask for forgiveness for my bad attitude and poor testimony as a Christian. He listened while he enjoyed his meal, but I could tell he was amazed at what I was telling him. He didn't make many comments, but I could tell he was really pleased with the change he saw in me. I feel much better now and want to try very hard to be a better wife. My desire is to bring my husband to the Lord."

We prayed together and thanked the Lord for His goodness and faithfulness. He had done a great work in Ester's life—a simple woman, but one who loved the Lord and longed to do His will.

She asked her husband to accompany her to church, and he agreed. Her testimony did not only extend to her husband, but also to others who were living in the same house. They saw a great change in her from an angry and bitter woman to a woman with a sweet spirit.

A few years ago, the Lord called Ester home after a long battle with cancer. She is now with the Lord, rejoicing in Him. No more suffering and tears for her, but pure joy in the Lord's Presence!

8

The Empire Strikes Back

The Christian and Missionary Alliance was not directly involved in the events that took place in the Seng Valley, but our close links with other sister Mission societies drew us into it and made us aware of the fact that we were all involved in the same struggle: the battle to win Irian Jaya for the Lord.

In September 1968, Stanley Dale and Phil Masters, two missionaries belonging to the Regions Beyond Missionary Union (RBMU), trekked into the Seng Valley several days from their own stations to explore the possibility of opening an airstrip and outpost in one of the valleys between their respective stations. From the moment they entered the area, they met with resistance. The hostility of the people became so obvious that they decided not to return as planned to Phil's station, but push on to Stan's station. However, on their way out, they were ambushed by armed warriors who killed them both and hacked their bodies to pieces. The full story is told in Don Richardson's marvelous book *Lords of the Earth*.

It was believed initially that the people who had a reputation for cannibalism had eaten the men, but Richardson disputes this in his book. (Later evidence confirmed, however, that parts of the bodies were cannibalized.) When the word was spread by way of two-way radio (that was the means by which all missionaries kept in touch with the MAF airplanes, with one another and with the outside world), everyone was in shock. We had lost two brothers in this war against the powers of darkness.

Vida Troutman, the first missionary to receive us in Enarotali when we arrived, had been sick, off and on, with attacks of malaria. The Troutmans had moved from Enarotali to Gakokebo, the village where we had spent more than two years during our first term. A new missionary couple, Paul and Jeannie Burkhart, were also stationed there for language study. Jeannie was a registered nurse.

On Friday evening of December 27, 1968, Vida became desperately ill. Since no planes were flying on Saturday, we had not turned on our two-way radio and consequently were unaware of Vida's critical condition. Early Monday morning an unscheduled MAF plane landed on our airfield in Kebo. The pilot reported that Vida had passed away on Sunday evening. Vida dead! How could this be? She was in her early fifties, a seasoned missionary who could not be replaced in the work at the Wissel Lakes.

THE EMPIRE STRIKES BACK

Two days later, we flew over to Enarotali for the funeral. It was December 31. Small single-engine airplanes with people from other Missions came in from all over the island to pay their last respects to Vida. The cemetery was on top of a hill from which we could overlook Lake Paniai and see the beginning of the high mountain range that leads up to the highest peak in Southeast Asia, Puncak Jaya, over 16,000 feet.

As the simple ceremony progressed, the weather grew ugly. High dark clouds closed off the pass that the planes would have to traverse to return the guests to their places of service. The passes to the east and to the north also filled up rapidly. We would have to find a way to sleep more than twenty guests. One of our Kapauku pastors gave a moving testimony about Vida's life, and with tears in his eyes stated that he thought that when missionaries died their bodies would be flown back to their own country. He was deeply touched by the fact that Vida was laid to rest in the earth of their country.

After the ceremony, we hurried down to the airstrip before the approaching rain could overtake us. On the way, one of the pilots told us that an MAF airplane was missing. The MAF bookkeeper and his family were flying from the south coast of the island to a station in the mountains. The pilot had last reported going through a pass called the South Gap. After that no further word had been received.

In view of the bad weather, none of the single-engine planes would be able to go up and begin a search. Only the Aerocommander, a twin-engine plane, that could fly at higher altitudes, left. Since

Kebo was still visible across the lake, it was decided that half of the guests would fly with us to Kebo and spend the night there. The other half would be put up in the two mission houses in Enarotali. We celebrated the strangest New Year's Eve ever, with more than a dozen guests in our home. All of us found our thoughts drifting to a place somewhere in the eastern highlands where a plane had probably crashed. The evening was spent in prayer and song. Finally, everyone drifted off to sleep.

The next morning, Pablo Pontier was the first pilot to leave Kebo, right at the crack of dawn. Shortly afterward, the other planes left, taking all the guests with them. New Year's morning found us with our ears glued to our two-way radio, following the airplanes as they went on their search. At about 9:30 a.m., Pablo reported that he had spotted the burned out wreckage of an airplane on the hillside in the Seng Valley, the same area where Phil and Stan had been murdered three months earlier. No survivors were spotted.

In order to reach the spot, a helicopter would be needed. At that time, MAF in Irian Jaya did not possess a helicopter. One was requested from Papua, New Guinea. When it arrived, it was confirmed that the plane had flown into the side of a mountain, killing the pilot and the Newman family instantly. Only Paul Newman, the nine-year-old son, could not be located.

Just when the helicopter was about to leave, a little white boy was seen running from the other side of the valley. It was Paul. When the plane crashed, he had been sitting in the back next to a small cargo door. He managed to climb out through that door and, as the plane caught fire and exploded, he ran for his life straight into the village of the killers of Stan and Phil. An older man in the village took him into his hut and protected him. When Paul was rescued, the people of the Seng Valley sent word to the outside world that they wanted to hear about the Jesus Way.

The death of two missionaries and the crash of an airplane became the blood of the martyrs, the seed of the Church. All of a sudden the Word of God started to sprout, grow and bear fruit in this valley of cannibals. "Precious in the sight of the LORD is the death of his saints," says David in Psalm 116:15. The Lord was willing to pay a high price for the souls of the Yali people in the Seng Valley.

Not only did the year 1969 open with this tragedy, but it turned out to be a year of continuing major attacks. Irian Jaya had now been under Indonesian administration under the auspices of the United Nations for almost five years, and the date set for the plebiscite, The Act Of Free Choice, as it was called, was rapidly approaching. Looking back on the event with the eyes of a Westerner used to democratic principles, the way the plebiscite was held did not leave much room for choice. There was not going to be a popular vote. That, in fact, would have been difficult in a country where most of the population was still illiterate.

Instead, a council of representatives of the people was formed, which consisted of people handpicked and duly bribed by the authorities. There would still be a vote, but it would be a vote that represented the deliberations and conclusions of an assembly rather than a vote of the people. This would result in an almost 100 percent consensus that Irian Jaya ought to be incorporated into the Republic of Indonesia.

However, the people of the Kapauku tribe living in the Wissel Lakes area had their own way of casting their vote. Small groups of people would come to our house in Kebo, usually after dark, to tell us that the people were making plans to drive the Indonesians out of their territory. We were told that they had chased out the Japanese during World War II, and the same would happen to the Indonesian soldiers and government officials. These people, just coming out of the Stone Age, had little or no understanding about the issues that determined the outcome of the Second World War. They had never heard of a man by the name of General MacArthur. They thought that the war had been won with bows and arrows.

We knew their efforts would be futile, but any advice we gave fell on deaf ears. The Kapauku, of course, did not succeed in chasing out the Indonesian government, but they managed to make life very miserable for those in power. The mountainous interior of the island was still inaccessible, except by small aircraft. There were no roads connecting the coastal area with the interior. All connections with the outside world depended on the versatility of airplanes and the condition of the small airfields. The Kapauku understood this, and they proceeded to sabotage the airstrips.

Beginning with the ones farthest removed from the government center, Enarotali, they closed one airfield after another by digging trenches across the strips or by planting trees or fence posts in the middle. We got word every day about airstrips that had been closed. It was like the approach of a thunderstorm.

One morning in May, I heard that the airfield at Enarotali across the lake from Kebo had been made unusable by seven ditches that had been dug across it. I realized what this meant. The only place that planes could still land in the Wissel Lakes area was our little airfield in Kebo. It was therefore predictable that Indonesian troops would be dropped off in Kebo, and a full-scale war would break out on our very doorstep. And there would be nothing we could do about it!

In the ensuing battle, people would be killed or wounded. We would not even be able to give medical help to any casualties. If we would treat a wounded Indonesian soldier, the tribespeople would consider that we were on the side of the government, and we would find the door closed to the preaching of the gospel in the future. If we would give first aid to wounded tribespeople, the Indonesian government would kick us out of the country. The only reasonable thing we could do was to withdraw. Two Indonesian families who were teaching at the Kebo Bible School would be evacuated first.

We called for an MAF airplane to fly those two families out to Nabire. Janine and I left on the last plane. Our children were all away at school in Sentani. As we left, I pleaded with the people not to dig ditches across the airstrip. If they wanted to make the strip unusable, they should use trees and fence posts. They promised they would not dig.

We left for Nabire and later went on to Pyramid to the conference grounds operated by the Mission. After about six weeks, the children joined us on vacation, but since we could not go back to Kebo, we all stayed at Pyramid. One day, we received a radio message from the Indonesian military asking us to return to Kebo. Indonesian soldiers had occupied the village, and we were told it would be safe for us to return. We had never been in danger; the uprising was against the Indonesian government, not against us as missionaries.

So, early on one beautiful June day, our whole family boarded an MAF plane and flew back to Kebo. Fence posts and trees had been removed by Indonesian personnel, and our plane landed without incident. The pilot was in a hurry, having a full flying schedule ahead of him, so as soon as our luggage was unloaded, the plane took off. It wasn't until he had left that we realized that things were not normal. Usually the landing of an airplane drew a crowd of people to the strip. There was only one lonely soldier with a gun.

As we walked the short distance to our house, we saw none of the villagers. Our house had been broken into, and someone had boarded up the front door. Once inside, we took a quick inventory. Because of the isolated conditions in the heart of the jungle, we always kept a good supply of canned foods. In case the plane could not fly in supplies for several weeks, we would not be forced to survive on sweet potatoes alone. The shelves of our pantry had been wiped clean. There was not a crumb of food in the whole house. Just before leaving for Nabire,

Janine had been going through the outfits that we had brought back from furlough the year before. It had not been easy to visualize how much our children would grow in the next four years and what sizes they would need. There had been four piles of clothes on the floor of one of the bedrooms. All those clothes were gone. There were no blankets left on the beds. The worst discovery, however, was that our two-way radio had disappeared.

So here we were, a family of six without any food, no spare clothes for the children, no blankets for the night and no way to tell anybody. I called the family together in the living room for prayer. I prayed a simple prayer along the line of, "Lord, if You don't help us now, we will perish." Immediately the sweet presence of the Lord descended upon us, and we all felt that God was not going to let us down.

As soon as I said, "Amen," someone knocked at the window of the living room. One of our friends, who had been hiding in the jungle with the rest of the population, had seen the plane land and came to see us.

"I know where your radio is," he announced. "We took it because we didn't want the military to get it." I told him that I would like to have it back as soon as possible. He disappeared and came back about half an hour later. When he handed me the radio transmitter, I realized what they had done. In their ignorance they had buried the sensitive equipment in a hole in the jungle with dirt on top. The dirt had been wiped off, but water was seeping out of the radio. They had not touched the 12-volt car battery that we used for transmitting. It had not been charged for over six weeks. Now, the only thing I could do was to hook up the set and try to transmit.

Miraculously, Paul Burkhart, who had gone back to Gakokebo shortly before we arrived home, picked up the signal. He could hear me weakly. When I told him our situation, his comment was: "You're lucky! The MAF plane just landed here. We'll get you some stuff and send it over." Before noon, the airplane landed again with food and some warm clothing, but no blankets.

But that was just the first miracle of the day. We found out that our house had been raided by the Indonesian military, not by the villagers. The troops had moved through the jungle, and they had just helped themselves. They never returned anything to us, with the exception of a pair of electric hair clippers. But around 4 o'clock that afternoon, one military man came with his arms full of our blankets which he handed to us without much comment. God saw to it that we had everything we needed to survive!

The situation was still very tense, however. Our arrival drew the people out of their hiding in the jungle, but the presence of the Indonesian troops was not conducive to a normal life. The soldiers also did not behave well. They were rough with the villagers, especially the women, and made themselves generally obnoxious. Their commanders were much more civilized, but seemed to have little control over their men. One major came over from Enarotali and apologized for what had happened to our property and to us. He told us he was a Christian himself. He felt ashamed. Finally, the troops moved out of the area.

The local population vowed that they would take up arms if they returned. Some tribal people who had worked for the police deserted, taking their guns with them. The locals were not heavily armed, but they had enough ammunition to ambush the troops if they dared to come back. And come back they did, running straight into the ambush. The number of people killed cannot be accurately established. Both sides inflated the statistics, but we could hear gunshots from our house, and it was obvious that a battle was raging up the river, about two hours' walk from our station. I did not want to expose our family to this trauma, so we decided to pack up and leave again. Since our annual mission conference was coming up in less than a week, we decided to fly immediately to Pyramid where the conference was to be held.

We left Kebo with very heavy hearts. The leader of the insurrection assured me that they were going to fight on to the bitter end and that all the mountain tribes in other valleys would eventually join this revolution. Was this the end of our ministry in Irian Jaya? Had all the years of labor by all the missionaries who had invested their lives in the Lord's work here been in vain?

The conference began with a day of prayer. I found myself in tears most of the time. The thought that we would have to leave Irian Jaya was unbearable. As we knelt down before the Lord and cast our burdens upon Him, the words kept returning to me: "But God . . . !" Then, all of a sudden, there was a breakthrough, and the assurance that the Lord was in charge and that He would take care of the insurrection at the Wissel Lakes came through loud and clear. The burden was lifted, and for the rest of the ten days of conference we were blessed by the messages brought by Don Richardson, who was our speaker that year.

The conference was honored by the presence of the commander-in-chief of the Indonesian army in Irian Jaya, General Sarwo Eddhie. He addressed us in perfect English and later spoke with me privately in excellent Dutch. He showed himself to be a very gracious person. I reported the conditions we had found upon our return to Kebo and the behavior of some of his troops. He expressed regret and apologies. He asked me to go back to the area and see if I could mediate. At that point, I could not promise anything, of course, not knowing what I would find.

At the end of the conference, it was decided that Janine and the children would go to Nabire, and I would make an exploratory trip to Kebo. I landed safely, and as soon as I arrived at our house, a delegation headed by the leader of the insurrection, Carl Gobai, came to speak with me. Carl had assisted Marion Doble with the translation of the Kapauku New Testament. He had left the Lord's work when he married a second wife. Carl had the gift of floating to the top whichever way the current was flowing. He had not initiated the revolt, but when the movement gained momentum, he took charge and, charismatic person that he was, people fell in line immediately. It was Carl who had told me before that the tribespeople were going to fight it out till the bitter end.

During our talk, I told Carl and the men who were with him that I sympathized with their desire for self-determination, but that I felt their cause was a hopeless one and that mostly innocent people would fall victim in their struggle for freedom. I suggested he surrender, and I offered to mediate. To my utter astonishment, he agreed without argument. He was willing to fly to Jayapura and surrender to General Sarwo Eddhie, he said. I could not help but see this as a result of God's intervention during our day of prayer at the beginning of the conference.

I made contact with the Mission office in Jayapura, and the next day a plane came in to pick up Carl. Two days later, he returned victoriously. The largest crowd I had ever seen on our airstrip awaited his arrival. Carl knew how to manipulate the crowd. He jumped from the plane, performed part of a tribal dance and shouted at the top of his voice: "The war is over!"

The audience understood this to mean that they had won the battle and that the Indonesians had agreed to leave their island. The opposite was, of course, the case, but Carl had his people where he wanted them, shouting deliriously for joy about what their leader had achieved. Then, using a fifty-five-gallon fuel drum as a platform, he elevated himself about the masses and spelled out the details of the surrender. All the guns they had in their possession should be surrendered to him. He would take care of them. The bodies of the slain Indonesian soldiers were to be handed over to the government, and life would return to normal after that. At this point it began to dawn on the people that they had actually lost the war. Some of the more clever ones started to shout, but Carl shouted them down. Anyone opposing what he had achieved would have to deal with him personally.

Somehow, that calmed the crowd. Then he played his best card: The general had asked him to become the head of the local government. Nobody realized at that point how clever their opponents had been. The Indonesians had sized up their man correctly. Being offered the post as head of government was a bait Carl could not resist. The fact that his Indonesian assistant would guide him in making important decisions made him a harmless but honorable figurehead. I have a picture of him, humbly presenting a gourd to Suharto, the president of Indonesia, who visited Enarotali a few months after Irian Jaya officially become a province of the republic.

Two days later all the guns were collected and flown out to Nabire. I was on the plane with Carl when they went. It was one of my most harrowing experiences in flying in Irian Jaya. As we took off, the oil pressure dropped as soon as the plane was airborne, and we almost crashed. We barely scraped over the edge of the fence at the end of the airfield. The pilot was able to cautiously maneuver the plane in such a way that we circled around and could land again without any major incident. The pilot opened the hood of the engine, located the trouble, and away we went. Janine, who had her ear glued to the radio, heard the pilot's report of taking off from Kebo. Then the radio went blank for almost two hours—some of the most difficult hours of her life. What a relief it was when she heard that the plane was safely in the air.

Janine and John were married on September 7, 1957 in Pâturages, Belgium. It was the perfect union of two nationalities, Belgian and Dutch, who are notorious for their inability to get along. We proved it could be done!

From L to R: Rev. Jan Knecht, Adriaan and Betsy Stringer, John and Janine Schultz and Rev. W. Könnemann, first on right, during the dedication service in Rotterdam. We and the Stringers were sent out to Irian Jaya by the Dutch Alliance as part of a group of missionaries which Rev. Könnemann had prayed would go in his place.

On December 1, 1957, our families gathered on the wharf to say goodbye. Janine's father wrote on the back of this picture: "Last tearful moments. A part of our life and our hearts moved away as the boat slowly left its moorings. That moment will forever remain engraved in our memories."

In Enarotali, on the shore of the Wissel Lakes, I carried Janine on my back to shore. We would often have to wade to dry ground.

The Mission residence in Enarotali was a log house. Built by Einar Mickelson in 1946, it was our home when we first moved to the Wissel Lakes.

This chapel at Enarotali was the first Alliance Church in Irian Jaya. The location commands an impressive view of the largest of the three Wissel Lakes where the Alliance work began under Walter Post in 1939.

Women do the fishing on the Wissel Lakes.

Walter and Viola Post were the first missionaries to walk from the south coast of the island to the Wissel Lakes. That was 1939. The trip took them 18 days. This picture was taken in 1982.

When Alliance missionaries landed with a float plane on the Baliem River to bring the gospel to the Danis, Elisa and his wife, Ruth, were the first Kapauku missionaries on board.

The Schultz kids in 1967. L to R: Mitch, Ruthy, JP and Viviane.

Rev. Theo Gobai was a brilliant young Christian and one of the first Kapaukus to study at Jaffray College in Makassar.

After the Posts left Kebo, the Bernards joined the staff along with three Indonesian teachers. L to R: Mr. Sohilait, John Schultz, Ed Bernard, Rev. Sumilat, Rev. Patty.

This is an aerial view of the Bible school and Mission residence at Kebo. The school was moved there from Enarotali in 1962 and was changed from a Kapauku school taught in the vernacular to an inter-tribal school taught in the Indonesian language.

Janine maintained good relations with the village people. Our medical ministry made us many friends.

Hond was a dear friend of our children and a good protector of our property. One night, he led me to the place where a chicken thief was hiding. Being caught while stealing chickens that belonged to Jesus eventually led the thief to accept Christ. God used Hond's nose to bring someone into the kingdom!

The Teacher Training Course was started in 1969 for the purpose of making the Bible school an indigenous operation. I specifically mentored several groups of five or six students.

The MAF planes were our only link with the outside world. There were no roads to connect us to the coast where supplies could be purchased. This picture was taken at Hitadipa.

After we moved to the coastal area of Nabire, our former students took over the job of running the Bible schools. Rev. Naftali Pigome was, until about 1999, the director of the Kebo Bible School.

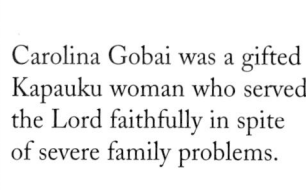

Carolina Gobai was a gifted Kapauku woman who served the Lord faithfully in spite of severe family problems.

Students in the Bible school at Kebo.

The Walter Post Theological School in Nabire consisted initially of five buildings: two classrooms with office, mimeograph room, library, two dormitories, a residence for the director, Rev. Sumilat, and the chapel.

Our move to Nabire and to the Walter Post Theological School was the challenge of a lifetime. The Lord was in it and guided step by step.

From the onset of the school, we endeavored to bring it under indigenous leadership. Less than three years after the school was started, Rev. Sumilat, left, took over as director.

I, along with Rev. Iyai, a superintendent, Rev. Sumilat and two local church leaders, participated in a dedication prayer for the graduates.

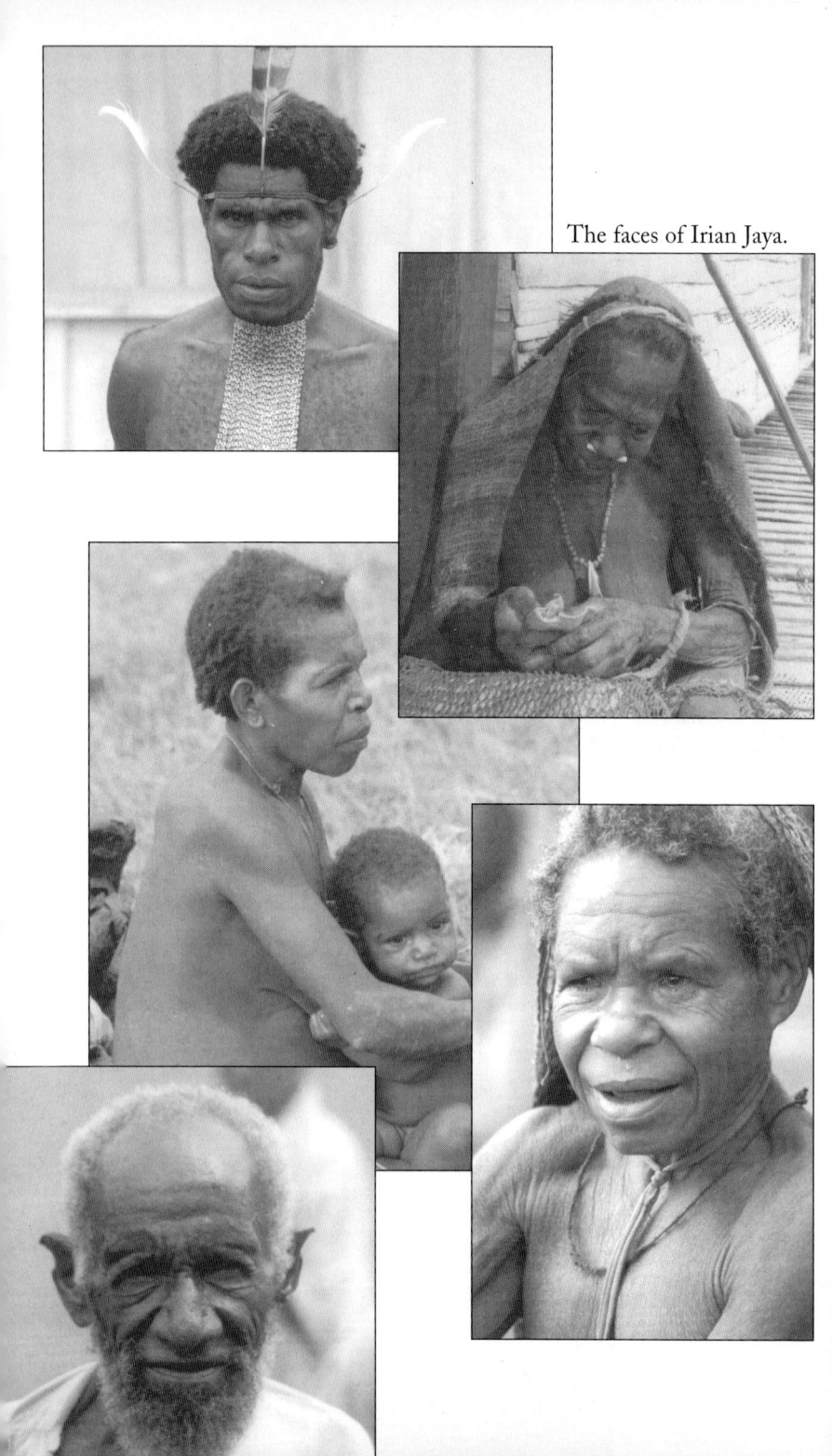
The faces of Irian Jaya.

The chapel at the Walter Post Theological School was constructed by Mission-trained local carpenters who did an excellent job.

This two-story building was a novelty in Irian Jaya. The first floor had rooms for married students, and the top floor housed single students, three or four to a room.

Many of the students were married. Their children added a lot of life to the campus.

Kegata was the most remote settlement in the Kapauku district. When a conference was organized by the national church, I was invited to bring morning devotionals and evening messages. It was during this conference that the national church decided to send their first missionaries to an unreached people's group.

Campus clean-up day. The jungle always tries to reclaim the ground taken from it. Students have to work consistently to keep the campus clean and livable. Joyful chants and Bible verses set to traditional tribal tunes accompany their labor.

We had dreaded the day of our final departure. But the warmth of love displayed at our farewell in Kebo in May of 1995 provided ample comfort for our tears.

The students of the Walter Post Theological School gave an elaborate feast for our farewell. Pork and sweet potatoes with greens were cooked in a pit on hot stones, native style.

Mitch and Elaine, with Travis
(seated, seven weeks before
his death), Brett and Breanna.

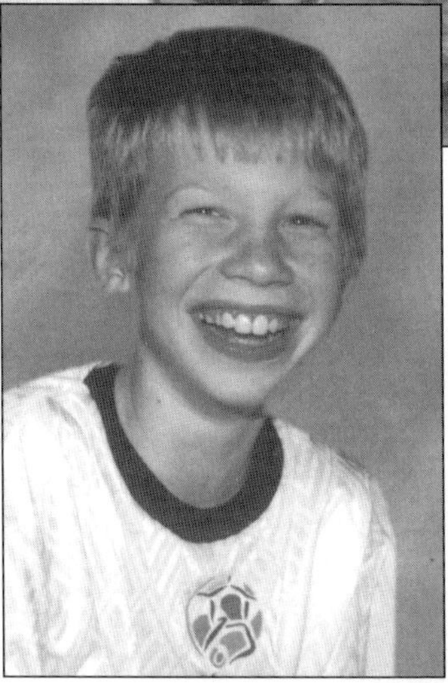

Travis at age 10.
The Lord took him
home on August 22,
1999 at the age of 12.

Viviane and Matt Miner,
with L to R: Maria, Max and Melanie.

Ruthy and Tim Hall, with L to R: Joshua, Sarah and Jason.

JP and Judy, with L to R: Alexis, Stephanie and Jordana.

John and Janine Schultz, 1998.

9

A Few Grams of Uranium

During the conference in Pyramid, mentioned in the previous chapter, a piece of legislation was enacted which was an act of faith. Even before there was any indication that the uprising would subside, we were reappointed to Kebo to head up the Kebo Bible School and to begin a teacher-training course for the purpose of forming a corps of indigenous teachers who could give pastoral training to their own people. It was supposed that the Bible school itself might not reopen for several months even if the political situation would clear up. A small group of young men would enroll in the teacher-training course and could easily be moved to a different location if the situation required it.

As it turned out, the Bible school reopened with little delay. Although the gardens had been neglected for several months, and sweet potatoes would not be readily available for some time to come, we were able, with the help of the Indonesian government, to purchase enough rice to keep the students fed.

Six young men were selected from our graduates to enroll in the new course. Some were chosen because of above-average scholastic achievement, and the rest in order to give a boost to other Bible schools taught in the vernacular languages of other tribal areas.

One of our friends in Holland asked us for a list of those students to be presented to prayer groups. Those profiles were later published in the *De Pionier*.

Reuben Magai is a young man from the Mapia, an area West of the Wissel Lakes. He is an intelligent fellow of about twenty-three or twenty-five. [A calendar was unknown before the coming of the white man, and until recently, none of the tribespeople knew the date of his or her birth.] He is married and has one child. His wife is expecting their second one. He enjoys the idea of teaching and is very eager to be trained well, but he is afraid to be original and keeps very close to his textbook.

Ben Yeimo is from the Kebo area. He is the oldest of the class. He is a gifted young man, about thirty or thirty-five, married with eight children. During the Dutch administration, he quit Bible school for a government job. He was greatly appreciated by the Dutch government, and they promoted him to be head of the district. After the Indonesian takeover, he gave up his job and returned to school to finish his Bible training. After graduating, he taught for a few years in a preparatory Bible school, and before we began our official training course, he taught some classes in the Kebo Bible School. When the course opened, he asked to be enrolled. He is strongly motivated and wants to study. He does very well in the classroom. He works hard, has a good sense of responsibility and is honest to the point that I felt free to put him in charge of the little store we run for our students a few times a week.

Lukas Edowai is about twenty-three or twenty-five years old. He is married and has two children. He is intelligent but rather nervous and, especially in the beginning, he lacked confidence. He has been doing much better lately, and in his student teaching he comes up with original illustrations. He gives the impression of being spiritually solid. A few months ago, he quarreled with his wife, and he came to tell me that he wanted to leave school. He said that it would not be honest to teach in a Bible school when his life was not in accordance with his words. He was very crestfallen about this and wept. I had a good talk with him and his wife. When we read Scripture together, the light broke through. . . . He comes from the Kamu Valley, immediately west of the Wissel Lakes.

Daud Iyai, who also comes from the Kamu, is by far the best student. He is a pleasant fellow with a very sharp mind. In the beginning he took things a little too casually, but lately he has applied himself more diligently, and he does excellent work. He has a wife and two sons. The younger of the boys has been very sick. Humanly speaking, we could expect a bright future for Daud and for the church in his area. That is why it is important to pray for people like him. They are often the target of the attacks of the enemy. Those are the students from the Kapauku tribe. The other two are from different tribes.

Daniel Alom is from the Damal tribe, from the Ilaga Valley, about seventy-five miles east of the Wissel Lakes. This is one of the highest plateaus in the mountain range, with much lower temperatures than the Wissel Lakes area. He was the first student from his tribe to come to the Kebo Bible School, which gives him a special status. He is a very sweet boy, a fine Christian and a thoroughly honest young man. But the Lord has not endowed him with the gift of brevity. He talks and talks and talks. His I.Q. is average. If he had belonged to the Kapauku tribe, we would probably not have accepted him in the course since he has a hard time in class. His Indonesian is pretty good, but I think that, eventually, he will probably have more of a ministry in his own tribal language. He will be quite suitable to teach in the Damal Bible

School in Beoga. He is in his early twenties, hasn't been married very long, and his wife just had a baby since they came to school here. Our children love Daniel, and so does our dog, which, in my opinion, is an indication of a healthy spiritual life!

Pilipus Zagani is a Moni. He is the only ordained pastor in the group. The Moni are undoubtedly one of the tribes that are hardest to reach. It is a miracle in itself that Pilipus has persevered, has finished his Bible training and has kept on walking with the Lord. He is one of only two Moni men who have achieved that. Experiences with other Moni students have been disappointing. For that reason alone, Pilipus needs our prayers. He is not very intelligent, but he is a good fellow. Like every other Moni, he has trouble with the pronunciation of some Indonesian words. Together with Daniel Alom, he has the lowest grades in class. But I have good hopes that the Lord will be able to use him in His harvest field. He is married, has three children and is probably about thirty years old.

Looking back over the years, I realize that not all of these first students of our Teacher Training Course have made lasting contributions to the growth of the church. Reuben Magai did quite well. He became a staff member of the Kebo Bible School and did an excellent job. When once, unexpectedly, I had to leave Irian Jaya for a medical emergency in our family, he took over the administration of the school and kept it running smoothly. Harold Catto, our field chairman at that time, came to Kebo for a school board meeting and found to his amazement that Reuben had prepared all the material for the agenda of the committee meeting and was able to back up everything with figures. He was later elected as president of the National Church, in which capacity he served for several years. He was accused of some wrong dealings that took place during his administration and left his position under less than favorable circumstances. When we left Irian Jaya in 1995, he was pastoring one of the churches in the city of Nabire.

Ben Yeimo did not persevere, either in his ministry as a teacher or in his walk with the Lord. He left the ministry and even quit going to church. His wife is a very solid Christian who holds the family together. When I last met Ben, he was disillusioned and bitter.

Lukas Edowai taught for several years and then moved to Nabire where he planted a church and built up a good work. He went back to the mountains, and got involved in a syncretistic movement which linked the gospel to elements of a cargo cult. When I saw him last, he was full of questions and seemed rather confused.

Daud Iyai, the most brilliant of my students, turned out to have a strong confrontational streak in him. He managed to get himself in trouble in every post he held. He was elected as district superintendent of the Nabire district, a post he held for four years. After he left this post, he lost his positive testimony as a servant of the Lord.

A FEW GRAMS OF URANIUM

Daniel Alom has proven himself to be a most faithful and sweet minister of the gospel. He went back to his area, taught Bible school, became district superintendent of his area, member of the Synod of the Alliance Church in Irian Jaya and is still going strong for the Lord.

Pilipus Zagani suffered much from the early death of his wife. He returned to his tribe and later moved to the Nabire area where he served in various capacities.

This may sound disappointing, and it would make one wonder how effective the teacher training course was. It must be remembered, though, that the percentage of students who graduate from a Bible school and end up having an effective ministry for the Lord is generally rather low. A Bible school or college has been compared to a uranium factory. Loads of ore are brought in and only a few grams of pure uranium come out. I must add that this first training course was not the only one that was ever held in Kebo. After the first group graduated, I taught another one, and some of those students have had rich ministries in the church. After our departure from Kebo, Elze Stringer taught at least two more courses, and several of those students have become Bible school teachers.

For me, the four years spent with these two groups were some of the richest in my experience. I learned probably more than my students did. I discovered that they had difficulty looking at a text and distinguishing between elementary truths and secondary points. They tended to get bogged down in details. We had no textbooks at our disposal and, to my knowledge, no one had ever tried to teach these kinds of skills to people coming out of the Stone Age using the Indonesian language. So I had to create my own textbooks as we went along.

We studied sermons and articles by well-known preachers and writers, and then we tried to analyze what the text said. The students had to prepare lessons that they would teach in the Bible school. I would help them with their preparations. They would teach some of the classes I had taught before. Their lessons would be taped, or I would sit in their class while they taught. Then we would get together and discuss the outcome of the lesson, and I would compliment them on what they had done well and help them to see the negative points in their delivery. They did not like the tape recorder in front of them. They called it "Mr. Schultz's little black spy." It was, however, very helpful to them.

One of my most outstanding students in the second teacher training course was a young man by the name of Matius Magai. He came from one of the most remote valleys in the interior of the island, from the village of Kegata. I remember the first time I met him and tested him for entrance to the Bible school. Matius immediately showed himself to have a sharp analytical mind and a pleasant and engaging way of dealing with people. He was an excellent preacher and gave rich sermons filled with illustrations from his own culture. I learned more about the culture of the Kapauku tribe from Matius' sermon illustrations than from any other source. Matius and I became very close friends.

When, in later years, the missionaries left Kebo, Matius became the director of the Kebo Bible School. He came for one year to Nabire for an upgrading course and then went back to his original post. His stay in Nabire proved to be disastrous for him. He had several attacks of malaria which gave him cirrhosis of the liver, and he died prematurely. I felt his departure very keenly.

September 24, 1969: Today we started with the classes for the six students of the Teacher Training Course. The work fascinates me, since it is uncharted territory. The fellows are some of the smartest compared with all of our former Bible school students, and it is a joy to teach when students are eager to learn. One student, Daniel Alom from the Ilaga Valley, has not yet arrived.

September 28: Although today is Sunday, I had to get out of bed at 5:30 a.m. The students had killed a pig in the school gardens, caught in the act of eating their sweet potatoes. It turned out to belong to one of the village chiefs. He insisted that the students eat the pig, and deposited it on the path in front of one of the dormitories. If the students had consented, according to the custom of the tribe, they would have had to pay for the pig. So they took the pig, and dropped it in the man's own garden. This made him very angry, and he threatened to return the aluminum roofing the school had given him the year before as payment for the ground he had given us.

When we came out of church, we realized that the man had changed his mind and had decided to eat the pig himself, because we saw smoke rising from the roof of his hut. In the afternoon, I learned that, during the worship service, he had gone to the dormitory and had stolen a pig that belonged to one of the students, one that the fellow had brought from his distant village to sell and pay his school tuition. I was indignant and decided to write about it to the head of the local government in Enarotali.

October 3: The arrival of the plane with medicine sent to us from the Netherlands gave us reason for rejoicing. We decided to share some with the local government male nurse who had recently opened a small clinic in the village. His shelves are usually empty, and if he cannot help the people, they come to us anyhow. The assistant head of the local government came over to settle the dispute about the pig in the school garden. We won the case, the student got his pig back, but we refused to accept the fine that was imposed upon the village chief. Living in peace with one's neighbors is more important than money.

October 6: The twin-engine plane of MAF from Sentani arrived. This plane is actually too heavy for our small and fragile airstrip, and mud splashed all over the plane. The load was a beautiful three KVA diesel generator that should provide our campus with electricity for the evening hours. Now all we need before we will be in business is diesel fuel and electrical cable.

October 8: One of the student's wives had been in labor since Saturday. Janine called me from my class in the afternoon, because it seemed that the placenta was coming out first. We called the Mission doctor over the radio, and we prayed. The Lord answered immediately. The baby was born normally.

October 17: The Burkhart family was on their way back to their station in Tigi, but the plane could not land since the airstrip was halfway under water. So they came to Kebo.

October 20: I had to fly to one of the Mission hospitals, about one hour's flying time from Kebo, since I had cut the tendon of my finger while repairing the grass mower for the airstrip. The doctor was not convinced the tendon was actually severed, and he only stitched my finger back together.

October 22: During morning recess, the students came to tell me that the sweet potatoes in their gardens were finished. We prayed for a solution to this problem, and I called our field chairman, Harold Catto, over the two-way radio. I will try to go to Nabire tomorrow and, if possible, buy fifty bags of rice. Food distribution is actually the indigenous church's responsibility, not the Mission's, but there is a general scarcity of food at the moment. I don't think we should distribute rice free of charge though. We need repairs on our airstrip. I will give some time off to the students so they can earn their rice every day by doing repair work.

October 23: The pilot from Nabire came to pick me up at 8:15 a.m. Upon arrival in Nabire, I went to see the head of government, and he allowed me to buy sixty bags of rice. I paid for the rice and was able to leave immediately with ten bags and fly back to

Kebo. Before 12 o'clock, I was home with food for the hungry. The students were grateful, and they were even more grateful when we had electric lights that night for the first time in the history of the school.

October 25: Very busy the whole day with entrance exams for young men who want to enter the Bible school. About seventy candidates showed up from the immediate area.

October 27: Something went wrong with the generator, and the lights went out. The rectifier had burned out. Back to our old kerosene lamps! It will take time before we will be able to have electricity; the part has to come all the way from Australia. James says: "Consider it pure joy, my brothers, whenever you face trials of many kinds, because you know that the testing of your faith develops perseverance" (1:2-3). How do you do that in the jungle of Irian Jaya when all the lights go out?

10

Hond and Some Lessons in Forgiveness

Kebo was a beautiful place to live, with a climate that could be called ideal for a location only a few degrees below the equator (warm but not hot during the day and cool at night), but it was very isolated. The only reasonable way to get there was by air. There were no roads connecting the Wissel Lakes with the coastal area, and trekking through the jungle would have meant a very strenuous, ten-day effort. So, except for some food items that were locally available, everything we needed had to be flown in by MAF plane. This was one of the reasons we decided to raise a few chickens so we could eat fresh eggs from time to time.

One night, the chickens woke me up in the middle of the night with loud and uncharacteristic cackling noises. Janine woke up also. We decided that someone was trying to steal our chickens. I jumped out of bed, got a flashlight and went outside. Our full-bred

German shepherd dog, Hond, was chained to the doghouse close to the kitchen door. I told Hond that someone was stealing our chickens, and that she better come along to catch the thief.

When we arrived at the chicken coop, we found the door open and feathers all over the place, but no trace of a thief. I beamed my flashlight around the yard without seeing any clues. I suggested to Hond that we call off the search and go back home. She looked at me with her big brown eyes, which seemed to say: "You humans are dumb! Can't you smell him?" She put her sleuth's nose to the ground and started following the scent she had picked up. This led us to the fence that ran around the school campus.

Since the fence was rather high, and there was a ditch on the other side, I decided not to climb over myself, but to go out of the yard and have a look on the other side of the fence. Hond followed joyfully. We found three chickens with their necks wrung in the ditch. Evidently, we had been closer on the heels of the thief than I expected. He had apparently made a run for it when we entered the yard and disposed of the evidence, probably planning to pick it up later.

Obviously, we had beaten him to it, so I took the chickens and wanted to go home. The man was no doubt miles away by now. But Hond was not ready to give up yet. Her nose went again to the ground, and she led me to the river, sniffing up and down a tree that was leaning over the water. Evidently, the burglar had considered hiding in the tree and, after climbing partway into it, decided against staying. Our path went upstream from there until Hond stopped at a dip in the ground overgrown with reeds and started barking fiercely.

When I shone my flashlight on the reeds, I saw the foot of a man sticking out. I summoned him to come out; he complied. There was something in his attitude, however, that seemed to suggest that I would have a hard time connecting him to the crime. The only evidence I had was Hond's nose and the fact that the man was hiding in the bushes, neither of which would stand up in court. I whispered in Hond's ear, and she immediately stretched herself full length, put her front legs on the thief's shoulder and her snout in front of his nose, then she let out a fierce bark. The change in the man's attitude was remarkable. He began to tremble and quickly assured me that he would pay me for the chickens.

By this time, we had made enough noise to wake up the students of the Bible school. Soon a crowd who wanted to know what was going on surrounded us. I showed them the three dead chickens and told them what the man had done. The students began arguing with the burglar.

"What's getting into you? Don't you know what kind of place this is?" they asked. "This land belongs to Jesus, and those chickens are Jesus' chickens. Of course, you were caught trying to steal chickens that belong to Jesus!" I had not looked at the matter from that angle, but I could not argue against it either. The students gave no credit to Hond.

The man repeated his assurance that he would pay and, swinging his net bag from his shoulder to his chest, he fished out one cowry shell, which he handed to me. Having no idea what the value of this kind of cultural currency would be, I asked someone: "Is this enough for three chickens?" Their silent nods made me understand that I was getting a very good deal. I accepted the shell and told the man to go home. With a furtive glance at Hond, he disappeared in the dark. I never saw him again.

A long time after that event, our carpenter, the repairman who kept the campus of the school in good condition, asked me if I had ever heard the rest of the story. I hadn't. It appears that the thief was impressed by the information the students had given him, that there was a certain Jesus who owned chickens one ought not to steal because he would certainly be caught. When the thief arrived in his village early that morning, he asked some of his friends about Jesus. Some people in the village had frequented a church in the area. They suggested that he go to church and find out for himself. Wanting to know who this Jesus was, whose chickens one couldn't touch, the man started going to church. It took a while before it dawned on him that Jesus was not just an important man who owned chickens, but that He was the Creator of heaven and earth who had come down to pay for man's sin and the sins of anyone who tried to steal a missionary's chickens. This man became a believer and was later baptized.

I wished I could have shared my joy with Hond and could have told her what an important role she had played in a man's salvation.

February 3, 1970. This year, I am a member of the field executive committee which meets in Beoga this time. The reason I mention it is that the committee decided to appoint another teacher to the Kebo Bible School to replace Willem Patty, who left. The appointee is Jan Lesnussa, the son of the couple who were murdered during the Obano uprising in 1956.

(written by Janine)

Young Jan Lesnussa was enjoying a fun time with his Kapauku friends in Enarotali, blissfully unaware of what was going on across the lake in the small village of Obano. Soon, his small world would collapse when the news came that both his parents and several of his friends and siblings had been killed in a native uprising.

November 3, 1956, was an important day in the history of the Alliance in Irian Jaya. Rev. Robert Chrisman, who was the Area Secretary for the Far East, had come for a field visit. In Obano, along with other missionaries and nationals, he took part in the dedication of a new aircraft owned by the Alliance and flown in by Ed Ulrich. Following the ceremony, Chrisman and the missionaries left by boat for Enarotali. None of them was aware of the trouble that was brewing among the people in Obano.

The following day, Sunday, November 4, a group of Kapauku warriors attacked the Mission station in Obano, leaving a trail of destruction. The Lesnussas, along with two Indonesian school children, Martha Rumaseb and Robert Paksoal, were shot by deadly arrows. The people, crazed by the smell of blood, went on a rampage, burning the Mission property and destroying the new airplane. Jan Lesnussa, about nine years old at the time, was suddenly left an orphan. Another Indonesian family adopted him and took care of him till he was old enough to leave Enarotali for further studies.

At an early age, Jan gave his heart to the Lord and felt His call to the ministry. It was a very clear call: "Jan, I want you to take your parents' place and serve Me in Irian Jaya." To get ready for the ministry, Jan went to college in Makassar, Indonesia. There, he met Annie, who became his wife and life partner in ministry.

Their first assignment was teaching in the Bible school in Kebo where John and I had been teaching for several years. What a joy and privilege it was to work with Jan and Annie. From the beginning, Jan showed a great love and respect for the people in the village. In return, they loved and respected him. They called him Les Yokame (Les' Boy).

In 1973, an evangelistic team of the Kebo Bible School went on a visit to Obano for special meetings. Jan Lesnussa was asked to go along and be the speaker. To everyone's amazement, he accepted the invitation. At the end of one of the meetings, a man came forward, holding two arrows in his hand.

"These two arrows were used to kill your parents," he told Jan. Immediately, Jan approached the man, hugged him and said that he forgave him. This incident made a deep impression on the congregation, and it spoke more than any sermon Jan might have preached.

To this point, these people had only believed in revenge—"eye for eye and tooth for tooth." Here they witnessed and experienced the real meaning of forgiveness. It became a live object lesson for the people. It was something they would not soon forget. For a long time, sitting in their huts around the fire, they would reminisce about what they had witnessed. Jan's testimony had a great impact on the life of the Kapauku.

(written by John)
We met Rev. Chris Paksoal shortly after our arrival on the field. After we had settled in Enarotali, we flew to one of the smaller Wissel Lakes, Lake Tigi, where another Dutch couple, the Stringers, worked. While there, we attended a tribal pig feast on the other side of the lake. Paksoal pastored a rather large tribal church about half an hour's walk from the area where the feast was held. He also taught a school for tribal children. We were invited to their very hospitable house for a delicious Indonesian meal.

Both Paksoal and his wife were natives of the area of Ambon, one of the principal islands in the Moluccas, the Spice Islands of the Indonesian archipelago. At an early age, Paksoal knew that the Lord had called him for full-time ministry. He received his training at the Alliance Bible School in Makassar. When Paksoal completed his studies, the Lord called him and his young bride to go to Irian Jaya, then called Dutch New Guinea. When we met him, he and his wife had already served the Lord faithfully for many years. Their son, Robert, had been killed in the native uprising in Obano, but they made the supreme sacrifice to the Lord without wavering.

In 1963, when the church in Irian Jaya became independent, Rev. Paksoal was chosen to become its president. His responsibilities took him to many places around the country, visiting churches, encouraging pastors, baptizing new believers. Several years ago, the Alliance invited him to be one of the speakers during our annual conference. In one of his sermons, as part of a moving testimony on the meaning of forgiveness, he related the following story.

One day, he received an invitation to go to Obano to minister to the people there and to hold a baptismal service. With apprehension, he accepted. He still had vivid memories of what had taken place during the uprising. His beloved son and several of his friends had lost their lives at the hands of angry natives.

When he alighted from the small airplane, several of the native people came forward to greet him. He had a hard time being pleasant to them. A tremendous struggle was going on in his heart. All he could remember was angry crowds killing his son. How could he shake hands with these murderers? Would he ever be able to forgive them? The Lord began to teach him a lesson in forgiveness, reminding him of His own ultimate sacrifice and asking him to forgive also.

During the baptismal service a man came to him and confessed that he had taken part in the killing of Robert. He asked Paksoal for forgiveness.

"The Lord has forgiven me, will you also forgive me?" he asked.

"How can You ask this from me, Lord?" Paksoal prayed. "This is too hard!"

The Lord answered him, "With My strength, you can do it. Just try. Tell the man you will forgive him."

Finally, Paksoal shook hands with the man and told him he was forgiven. The Lord had taken away all anger and bitterness and replaced it with a great inner peace. Paksoal then proceeded to baptize the man who had killed his son.

This act of forgiveness impressed the people deeply, and many gave their lives to the Lord as a result of this testimony.

11

Rebellion, Revival and Readjustment

February 1, 1971: Today was the beginning of the second semester in school. Actually, we should have begun last week, but when I returned from a committee meeting in Sentani, on January 26, it turned out that over half of our students were sick with the flu, so we decided to close the school for a week.

One of the Moni students had been angry with his wife and had given her a severe beating. I felt that I should give him some sort of punishment for that, but this morning we found out that he had taken off to Enarotali. His wife and baby are still here, but their blankets and clothing have disappeared.

February 3: This afternoon we had a brief hailstorm. This is the first time I have seen this phenomenon here; since we are near the equator, I was amazed, and so were the students.

February 8: A young Dutch missionary couple, Pieter and Nel Akse, arrived today to study Indonesian at our station. They plan to stay here at least till July. We had wanted to receive them in a worthy manner with a genuine Indonesian meal, but Grandma Sumilat, who is an excellent cook for such occasions, was still sick, and so the official reception had to be postponed a couple of days.

February 13: The Moni student who had disappeared has returned. At first he tried to tell me that he was right, but later he apologized, and humbly accepted his punishment which consisted of one week's community service, which is work in the school garden.

February 15: The students had come earlier to complain about food shortage. This is a real problem. The garden ground is impoverished and the sweet potato harvest becomes less every year. The Food and Agricultural Organization, a department of the United Nations, has given us a present of one ton of fertilizer, but thus far I have been unable to raise the money for the air freight. I advised the students to call Rev. Yunus Gobai, who is the representative to the school of the indigenous church, to ask him if the church could help. I explained to the students that the Alliance was not in a position to help, after which I left them alone to discuss the matter.

When they called me back, one hour later, they had not yet found a solution. One of the members of the student council was rather rebellious. He did most of the talking. I told the students that those who were really hungry were allowed to go home, but that the school would not be closed. Because they wouldn't be able to leave before the next morning, I insisted that they would attend the Indonesian language classes in the afternoon; otherwise, the teachers from the village schools, who come specifically to teach those classes, would come in vain. But there appeared to be a spirit of rebellion among the students and hardly anyone came to the classes. Those who had wanted to come were afraid of the others who had gone on strike.

February 16: The confrontation continued today. Nobody came to class except for one or two students, but nobody has gone home either. I talked again to the student council. The rabble-rouser of yesterday was, as I had suspected, the instigator of the strike. He permitted himself some very impolite utterances, first to me and then to Mr. Sumilat, one of the Indonesian teachers. Afterward, he came to apologize. I made no progress with the student council and decided to call a general meeting with all the students. In the culture of the tribal people, everything is decided by common consent; pushing one person's viewpoint avails nothing.

Mr. Sumilat and I decided to let the matter settle and closed the school till Monday. Those who had not gone home by Monday were supposed to come to school. In the evening, a group of students, mostly from the eastern highlands, met in our living room under cover of darkness to tell me that they were sorry things were going this way. They wanted to stay, but they were looking for an acceptable way to communicate this to the student council without losing face.

This kind of approach is difficult for a Western mind to understand, but I had the feeling that we were on the way to a more normal situation.

February 19: Two of the members of the student council, one of whom was the rebel leader, went to Enarotali to talk to the vice-president of the National Church. They came back with the promise that the church would give a sum of money, the equivalent of $100, to ease the situation. With this money I can buy a certain amount of rice for the students. It is not much, but it will probably be enough to last through Easter vacation. The blessing of all this is, in the first place, to make the students understand that independence and the right to have a say in school matters bring responsibility. It also indicates that the indigenous church is taking a greater part in the running of the school.

February 20: Our generator acted up in the evening, and we had to shut it down.

February 22: Spent most of the day with Pieter Akse taking the generator apart, cleaning everything and putting it back together. But the machine did not revive. We had to go back to our kerosene pressure lamps.

February 25: I had to leave for Jayapura for a committee meeting with Dr. King, the foreign secretary for the Alliance. The Cessna came to pick me up at 7 a.m. We first had to make a landing in Tigi to pick up a man who had broken his arm. When we landed, the patient was nowhere to be found. When he still didn't show up after a while, the pilot decided to leave. We landed next in Hitadipa and after that in Weri, a new airstrip in the Lakes Plain north of the central mountain range. It was a fascinating flight. John Wilson, a missionary from among the Dani tribe, had trekked to the place. He was told it would take him about five days, but it turned out to be a thirteen-day trek, and he had not had enough food with him for the extra days. Nobody ever looked so happy to see us as John Wilson!

The trip had not been without its dangers. We ferried John safely back to his station and to his wife. The inhabitants of the Lake Plains are nomads whom I had never seen before. Many people from the area have never seen a white man, and they have never heard the gospel. They wear a small piece of tree bark as an apron, instead of the gourd used by the mountain Papuans. They have their nostrils pierced with crooked pieces of bones of a bird.

From John's station we made two more landings, and then the clouds had started to build up, and the mountain passes were closed. We didn't make it to Jayapura, but had to spend the night at an MAF base.

March 1: After a short stay in Sentani, where I was able to see our children, and after the meeting with Dr. King, the plane brought me back to Kebo. My fellow passengers were John and Helen Ellenberger. John will hold special meetings with the students. After the first evening service, a large number of the students stayed for counseling. John and I talked with more than forty men, some of them with their wives. The majority had things to set right with the Lord. Others confessed to having lied or stolen things. It was a surprising but wonderful breakthrough. I was tired, but grateful when I finally went to bed at midnight. I had been up since 5 that morning.

The son of one of our students incurred serious burns when his mosquito net caught fire. We treat his burns daily, but he will have to be sent to the mission hospital for a skin graft.

March 2: The meetings have made a profound impression on our students. After the last service, there was hardly anyone who had not stayed behind for counseling or prayer. The Lord has been at work. We believe that the difficulties of the previous week were a preparation for this blessing.

January 1, 1972: Yesterday, we returned from a youth conference in Sentani, where I had the privilege of speaking seven times. More than 120 young people attended. The Lord blessed, and many dedicated their lives during the services. To return from this victorious atmosphere to Kebo, where everybody is down with the flu, is quite a change. We started the New Year with giving out medicine for about two hours. There was a large group of small children who had symptoms of diarrhea and vomiting which can easily become life-threatening.

January 7: Our fiberglass boat leaks like a sieve; the fiberglass is cracked in several places. Therefore, it would be unsafe to cross the lake with it. Our sons, J.P. and Mitch, accompanied me to the boathouse at the mouth of the river about an hour's walk from our house. When I came back home, I promptly felt sick myself. I concluded that I probably had the flu also.

January 12: We have trouble getting the school started after Christmas vacation. On the west side of the lake, fourteen students are waiting for a canoe that isn't there. None of the Moni students from the east have arrived yet. We decided to postpone the classes one more day.

January 13: Nel and Pieter Akse left today for Tangma. They were busy packing till late into the night. Most of their luggage will have to stay behind for the time being. The Cessna cannot take off with more than 850 or 900 lbs., which includes body weight.

January 15: Lost quite a bit of time trying to wrap the Akses' refrigerator in burlap bags. After that, went with the children to look at a little calf which was just born this morning. The flu is not over yet. J.P. came down with a fever today.

January 18: Our children left for school today. The plane didn't arrive until 1 p.m. That meant a whole morning of waiting. After they left, the house was terribly empty, and we felt a deep sadness. Once again, the Lord came to our side with His comfort.

March 30: The plane came at 6 a.m to take us to Sentani for our biannual vacation which we spend with our children at the M.K. school. We flew straight to Sentani and arrived about 7:30. The students were already in school, and we had to wait till 9 before we could see our family. Received word from the Mission's headquarters that we would be allowed to furlough in the U.S. this coming June.

April 1: The children began celebrating April Fools' Day at an unearthly hour by blowing trumpets, beating tin drums and throwing stones on the roofs of houses. In the afternoon we helped with the Easter egg hunt.

April 10: Left Sentani for Tangma, where Pieter and Nel Akse are now living. This place looks like the end of the world. A better example of the Stone Age would be hard to imagine.

April 17: Janine and I are in the Ilaga Valley to administer entrance exams to candidates for the Bible school. Completely unexpected word came over the radio this morning that Janine's father had passed away. The cable that was sent had taken a long time to reach us. We didn't learn what date he had died, but it seemed as though it was about two weeks ago. We had received a letter, dated March 3, in which he said he had been sick, but was doing fine. We are a little over two months away from our furlough when we would have seen him. This was very hard to bear for Janine. The Larsons and Ellenbergers, missionaries in the Ilaga, were very compassionate in their attempts to comfort us.

June 29: This is our last day in Kebo. Today we leave our station for furlough. These last weeks have been occupied with tying up loose ends, finishing little projects and packing. We are so exhausted that furlough seems to be the only reasonable solution. To top it, yesterday I came down with intestinal complaints and diarrhea, but fortunately I was able to keep working. The pilot who flies us to Nabire is Pablo, the same one who picked us up fourteen years ago to fly us to the Wissel Lakes for the first time. He landed about 8 a.m., and since we absolutely had to take all our luggage with us, and since the airstrip was still wet with morning dew, Pablo decided to take a minimum of gas. That would make the plane lighter for take-off. It would also mean that one of the tanks would run dry during the flight, and he would have to switch from one tank to the other in midair. Halfway, the engine began to sputter and quit. Janine and the children, who didn't know what was happening, had the fright of their lives, thinking that something was wrong with the plane and that we would spend our furlough in heaven. Obviously, this was not the case, and we landed safely in Nabire.

June 30: Circumstances were not favorable to celebrate Mitch's birthday. Nabire did not have any shops where we could buy presents, so he had to be satisfied with the promise that we would buy him something in Singapore where we were planning to spend a few days. We had made arrangements with our office in Jayapura, that MAF would fly us straight to Biak, on July 3, unless we could get on an Indonesian commercial flight. Since Nabire is situated at the beach of the Pacific Ocean, the children tried to water-ski with the little boat from the MAF pilot. Only Mitch succeeded in actually skiing. This accomplishment made him rightfully proud. We feel like millionaires in the midst of this tropical splendor.

July 2: After church and a quick lunch at the pilot's house, we went to the office of the Indonesian airlines where we succeeded in obtaining tickets for Biak. It was a tense moment when Viviane decided she had to go to the restroom at the airport and the pilot started one of the engines before Janine and she made it on board. I hadn't planned to go on furlough with only the two boys! However, they returned just in time. In Biak, we stayed at the hotel that was built by the Royal Dutch Airlines during the colonial days. It used to be a first-class hotel, but over the years it has gone into disrepair. Some restorative work has been done, and it is now halfway decent.

July 3: Having no other challenge, we wandered around in Biak, which is not an impressive kind of town. There is not much to see; the heat is usually stifling, but today the weather was tempered by a clouded sky. When we went to pick up our tickets, we discovered that Ruthy's ticket was made out for a four-year-old girl instead of our thirteen-year-old. I had to pay the extra fare from Biak to Jakarta.

July 4: After a short night of poor sleep, we awakened at 3 a.m. to get ready for our trip. The plane was due to leave at 5:30. We flew first to Menado, in Sulawesi, then to Makassar, and via Surabaya to Jakarta, a distance of well over 2,000 miles and about eleven hours! We had hoped to be able to arrange for a change of Ruthy's ticket at the Jakarta airport, since we were flying on the same afternoon to Singapore. We had notified the Alliance office in Jakarta, but nobody showed up. So we just boarded our next plane without anybody worrying about this big girl who flew on a four-year-old's ticket. In Singapore, a Mission representative supposedly had booked a hotel for us. I tried to phone him from the airport without any result. Here we were, exhausted after thirteen hours in the airplane, without a hotel. A taxi brought us to a hotel that seemed reasonable, but which turned out to be too luxurious for us, so we decided to spend only one night there.

July 5: Again, I tried to contact our Mission representative, but it was all in vain. The man had moved, and no one in the hotel could find his phone number. We ordered new tickets at the Royal Dutch Airline office, but I had to raise several hundred dollars to pay for the difference in Ruthy's ticket. Without our Mission representative, I knew I would be in very hot water. We moved to a cheaper hotel. Singapore is a wonderful city, with all the hustle and bustle of a metropolis, teeming with representatives of all the races of humanity. Shopping is also a pleasure, especially for someone who has been hiding four years in the jungle. Everything is tax free, and therefore very reasonable.

July 7: This morning I had the bright idea of looking in the phone book myself, and I found the missing Mission representative's number without any trouble! We agreed to meet somewhere in downtown Singapore, and so we were able to get our new tickets without any problem.

July 8: We had to vacate our hotel room at noon, or pay for another day. Since we had to be at the airport at 5 p.m., we decided to spend the afternoon in the lobby of the hotel. As we boarded the Dutch airplane at seven that evening, the stewardess handed me a Dutch paper of the day before. Suddenly, I realized that we were really on our way home. Four years in the jungle, among people who have barely come out of the Stone Age, had not prepared us for the problems of modern society we had faced during the last few days. We were learning that the Lord had the solution for each of them.

12

Tears Bigger than Mine

"In the shadow of glacier-capped Puncak Jaya, Irian's highest peak, steel jaws travel along the world's longest single-span tramway carrying 10-ton loads of ore across some of the most inaccessible terrain on earth. A huge refining mill and the world's longest slurry pipeline then transport the copper concentrate to a port on the malarial mangrove flats, fifty miles away on the coast." Thus reads an Indonesian travel guide.

We had heard about the mine, operated by Freeport Sulfur of Louisiana, and we knew that one of our missionary couples, John and Helen Ellenberger, who worked among the Damal tribe that occupies that area, had been called in by the company as consultants to advise them on matters related to communications with the tribal people. On one of those visits, John learned that the company was looking for a piano tuner to work on the instrument that stood in their recreation hall. He was told that they were planning to fly in a man from Australia to tune their piano! The expense would probably make the piano one of the most expensive keyboards in the world. But the company had no lack of finances.

John mentioned in passing that he had a missionary friend, a certain John Schultz, who tuned pianos as a hobby, and who also played Bach on the keyboard.

"Get the guy over here," he was told. So word came over our radio transmitter that Freeport invited me to come to Tembagapura (which means Copper City) to tune their piano. If I wanted to stay over the weekend, I would be welcome also to preach to the group of Christians in the city, both in English and Indonesian, and "please, give a Bach concert while you are at it." Janine would be welcome to come along also, and so was Ruthy, who had not left for school yet, since she had graduated from the school in Sentani and was now going to Dalat School, in Penang, Malaysia.

So, one beautiful, cloudless Saturday morning, the private helicopter came from Freeport to ferry the Schultz family from their station in the heart of the jungle to the modern Copper City. This was another culture shock. By now, we had adapted fairly well to life in the jungle at the edge of nowhere. However, within a little over twenty-five minutes we were dumped into the heart of a modern mining town—row upon row of concrete houses with central heat (which is needed at an altitude of over 6,000 feet), all equipped with electrical washers, dryers and refrigerators.

This transition was too abrupt, and it sent us reeling. There was a mess hall where we could eat food we hadn't tasted in years. There was a movie theater, a restaurant—all this on top of a mountain in the heart of the rugged jungle of Irian Jaya! The refrigerator in the guest house was stocked with delicacies which we were told were at our disposal.

Tuning the piano was an easy task, since, at that altitude, instruments are not subject to excessive humidity as they are at sea level. And preaching on Sunday to a church full of several hundred Indonesian Christians who did not have a pastor and were eagerly drinking in every word was an invigorating experience, as was the ministry to a smaller but very appreciative English-speaking group.

The piano recital was scheduled for Sunday afternoon. I had put together a modest program of classical music, and I was amazed to see the recreation hall almost completely filled. I did not expect to find such a hunger for culture in a remote mining town at the edge of the world. But there had been a misunderstanding. Most of the communication between John Ellenberger and the personnel of the mine had been done by radio, which, of course, is subject to static and fading in and out. John had said, "Bach Concert," but it was understood as "Pop Concert!" I lost my audience after the first two notes. One heavyset fellow from Alabama complimented me afterward, saying that he thought the music was very relaxing. He probably meant that he had slept through most of it!

The company was kind enough to invite me back, and over the years Janine and I made periodic visits to Tembagapura. The Alliance set up a rotating program in which one missionary would visit the town every month, and so our name was put on the list. Subsequent visits were, however, not done on the company's helicopter. MAF would fly us to Timika, an airfield on the south coast of the island, from which we would go up the fifty-mile mountain road by car. People with acrophobia should not travel that road. From the airport, slightly above sea level, the road goes up gradually for about twenty or thirty miles, but then it ascends with an amazing incline on what seems a razor's edge. From a distance it looks as if no vehicle could ever climb this unbelievably steep road. At some places, it is the only flat surface on the ridge. Picture the road! On the left is a 500-foot drop-off, and on the right is one of 1,000 feet or more. But at the end of the two-hour drive was a group of people who received us warmly and who were hungry for spiritual things.

Visiting Tembagapura three or four times a year was not only a welcome interruption of life in the jungle, but it was also beneficial for our health. The company's hospital was undoubtedly the best equipped on the whole island. American or other expatriate doctors were willing to help with any problem we might have and even provided medicine for the students in our Bible school. And then there was food that could only be bought in the exclusive store of the company. Our Indonesian friends were excellent hosts. Every time we arrived, they found an excuse to celebrate with a meal of exotic Indonesian dishes. On one occasion, I helped myself to a meat dish that did not look very appetizing to me, but I did not want to seem impolite, so I took some and ate it. It tasted horrible! The color was greenish, and so was the taste. It was also very spicy, more than anything I had ever eaten.

When I took my first bite, one of the guests looked at me in amazement and asked if I knew what I was eating. My answer was negative. Someone remarked: "I didn't know you like Scooby Doo!"

Not being versed in television programs, this didn't mean a thing to me. But Janine knew what it meant.

"You're eating dog meat!" she whispered.

My polite efforts came to an abrupt halt, and I put down my fork. When I got back home, I went to my dog and confessed what I had done, pleading ignorance and promising that I would never do it again.

Such a thing could never happen to us; it shouldn't happen to us. It might happen to other Christians, but we had tried to serve the Lord faithfully. . . . However, it did happen!

By this time, we had spent thirteen years in Kebo. I could hardly imagine any other form of ministry for Janine and me. When we left in June 1976, it was as if the Lord had to pry us loose. Actually, it was much more painful than that. The cause of our departure was the severe nervous breakdown of our younger son, Michel, also known as Mitch.

Mitch, then twelve years old, went back to the M.K. school in Sentani with his brother and two sisters in January of 1974, after Christmas vacation. He showed no unusual signs of anxiety, but after a few weeks we received word via the two-way radio that the presence of one of his parents was required since Mitch was very homesick. Janine went to see him, and as soon as she arrived, he was OK. After a few days, he told her that there was no need for her to stay, so she came home.

Almost immediately, Mitch sank into a deep depression. He would wake up early in the morning, then wake up his older brother, John Paul, and he would cry. After school, he would not mix with other kids, but he would sit by himself and cry. Mary Catto, the wife of our field chairman, realized that there was more involved than homesickness. So Janine flew out to Sentani again and brought him home. We decided that Mitch would stay with us until our vacation which we always spent with the children at Sentani.

As soon as we arrived for our vacation, he collapsed completely. The sight of the school campus brought back all the anxiety and depression that had been forgotten at home. The school nurse gave him some medication to which he had an adverse reaction. A mission doctor saw him, and told us that he was suffering from severe clinical depression. We had never heard of this and didn't know what to do. It was finally decided that Janine would stay in Sentani with our two other children, and I would take Mitch back to Kebo. However, back at Kebo, Mitch did not show any improvement, so we decided to make a trek through the jungle to Gakokebo, about one day's walk from Kebo. We had to cross the lake, walk for several hours and then cross another lake. Mitch's condition worsened as we walked. He cried and said he wanted to die. It was the most heartrending experience I had ever had. I felt it would have been comparatively easier to lose a child in death than to see him sink away in despair like that.

When we arrived at Gakokebo, Mitch was feeling so bad that we decided to call one of our doctors on the two-way radio. He recommended that Mitch be taken to the Mission hospital in the eastern highlands. A plane came the next morning to pick us up, and about one hour later we arrived in the northern part of the Baliem Valley. The doctor immediately recognized the symptoms and advised that we make arrangements to leave the country and go either to Australia or to Europe for a psychiatric evaluation. Within a few days, everything was arranged, and Mitch and I were on our way to Australia.

Bob Henry, the chairman of the Alliance work in Australia, had made all the arrangements for us. We were graciously taken in by a Christian doctor and his family, and a day or two later, we met with a Christian psychiatrist who advised that Mitch be hospitalized for about a month. We checked into a psychiatric ward, and I was given a bed in the same room with Mitch in order not to submit him to more anxiety.

We had left Kebo to go away for the weekend, but it was about four months before we returned. It took me a while to work through this shock. It was traumatic to be yanked out of a fruitful and enjoyable ministry to be set on an apparent sidetrack. I cried for my son. I cried for the work I had left behind without any warning. Why was the Lord doing this to us? Why did Mitch have to go through this agony? I prayed and cried for several days.

The answer the Lord gave was a most astonishing one, completely different from what I expected. The Lord did not answer my question as to why this happened, but He made me understand that my sadness about my son was a reflection of what He felt about Mitch. His sadness was infinitely greater than mine; His tears were bigger than my tears. I could not understand this, of course, but the truth worked like a balm on my wounded soul. I later discovered that C.S. Lewis must have gone through the same experience in his life. In his book, *The Magician's Nephew*, he tells the story of a boy named Digory who enters Narnia while Aslan is in the process of creating it. Digory had given in to some unhealthy curiosity which left the door open for an evil witch to enter Narnia. Digory's mother is at home very sick. Digory meets with Aslan:

> "Son of Adam," said Aslan, "Are you ready to undo the wrong that you have done to my sweet country of Narnia on the very day of its birth?" "Well, I don't see what I can do," said Digory, "You see, the Queen ran away and..."
>
> "I asked, are you ready?" said the Lion. "Yes," said Digory. He had had for a second some wild idea of saying "I'll try to help you if you'll promise to help my mother," but he realized in time that the Lion was not at all the sort of person one could try to make bargains with. But when he had said "Yes," he thought of his Mother, and he thought of the great hopes he had had, and how they were all dying away, and a lump came in his throat and tears in his eyes, and he blurted out: "But please, please—won't you—can't you give me something that will cure Mother?" Up till then he

> had been looking at the Lion's great feet and the huge claws on them; now, in his despair, he looked up at its face. What he saw surprised him as much as anything in his whole life. For the tawny face was bent down near his own and (wonder of wonders) great shining tears stood in the Lion's eyes. They were such big, bright tears compared with Digory's own that for a moment he felt as if the Lion must really be sorrier about his mother than he was himself.

God's tears about Mitch were bigger than mine!

Mitch responded well to treatment and was dismissed from the hospital after only two weeks instead of the one month that the doctor thought would be necessary. Janine came over with J.P. and Viviane. Ruthy was still at school in Penang. J.P. had just graduated from the eighth grade in Sentani, and I felt very bad that I had to miss his graduation. The Australian Alliance asked me if I would be willing to pastor a small Alliance Church while we were there. We rented a small house in Parramatta, one of the suburbs of Sydney. Mitch was on medication, and he had appointments with the doctor at regular intervals. He improved gradually, gained some weight and began to look like a different boy. His episodes of anxiety slowly decreased in frequency and intensity.

In August, barely four months after our arrival, the doctor told us that Mitch needed no further counseling sessions, but that he had to be on strict medication and should be reevaluated after one year. So after

Ruthy and J.P. left for Dalat School, we boarded a plane back to Jayapura.

Mitch was happy to be back home in Kebo, but life did not return to normal for him. He was unable to go back to school, so we home schooled him for one year. When, after that year he still was not ready, we began to rethink our future. We still had one year of our term left before furlough, but we asked the Mission for an early furlough and began to look for a place to settle in the United States where Mitch could be under further psychiatric care.

We heard that there was a Christian woman psychiatrist who was a member of the First Alliance Church in Atlanta. The pastor, Dr. Walter Sandell, arranged for some appointments with her and also found us a house. In addition to that, the Alliance Church granted scholarships in the church-sponsored Christian Academy for the three youngest children who were ready to go to high school. Ruthy eventually enrolled in Toccoa Falls College. They rolled out the red carpet for us in a most wonderful way, and we spent two and a half years on furlough in the Atlanta area. The church also sponsored our four children as foreign students to go to college.

As Dutch citizens, we were visitors in the United States. When we entered the country in New York, the immigration officer at JFK airport wanted to know how long we planned to stay. I told him that we were given a one-year furlough by our Mission. He answered that the rule was that visitors could spend six months in the U.S., and then they would have to leave.

"We would like to stay for one year," I said. He didn't look very accommodating but was willing to check with his boss. When he came back, he said: "I don't agree with this, but my boss says to give you one year." Before the year was over, the Alliance invited us to attend General Council which that year was in Calgary, Canada. We flew to Canada, not realizing the implications of our visa status.

Upon our return from Council, the immigration officer at the Newark airport wanted to know how long we wanted to stay this time. We tried for another year, but this officer proved to be even less flexible than her colleague in New York. Six months was all she would give.

My home assignment before the end of those six months led me to upstate New York. I told the pastor of one of the churches that I would love to see Niagara Falls. So we drove over, crossed the border into Canada, and I came back with another six months in my passport. Before this permit expired, the Lord arranged for the immigration laws of the United States to be changed. Extensions could be obtained at an office in Atlanta. It was no longer necessary to leave the country. So we stayed legally for two and a half years in the United States on a six-month visitor's visa. It was obvious that the hand of the Lord had been upon us.

However, because we had been out of Indonesia for more than one year, we had lost our Indonesian visa. At that time, the Indonesian government was unwilling to grant new visas. Once Mitch received medical clearance to return with us to Irian Jaya, we applied for a new visa. It took almost a year before it finally came through. When we received the phone call from our headquarters, telling us the news, I literally jumped up and down in the kitchen. We were going back! A large group of friends from the church saw us off in Atlanta on January 1, 1979.

For the first time in our lives we had to leave Ruthy and J.P. behind. Mitch and Viviane returned with us to Irian Jaya and on to Dalat School in Malaysia.

It took several years before I could begin to see the positive side of this terrible episode. First of all, we met a number of people who had gone through similar experiences and with whom we could share how the Lord had helped us. We also realized in retrospect that none of our children would ever have been able to enter the United States of America as foreign students without the sponsorship of the First Alliance Church in Atlanta. But most of all, the experience made Mitch into a well-balanced person whom the Lord could call into His ministry and make into a fruitful worker in His harvest.

Later in his life, it became obvious that the Lord had led him through deep waters in order to prepare him for the suffering his own family would go through. His wife, Elaine, almost lost her life in an emergency operation for the removal of a brain tumor in June 1998. And only four months later, their oldest son, Travis, age twelve, was diagnosed with a brain tumor. He passed away on August 22, 1999.

Sometimes it seems necessary to sow in tears in order to be able to reap with joy.

13

The Lord's Doing

When word was received about the new visa the Indonesian government had granted us, the National Church in Irian Jaya requested that we would not go back to Kebo, but relocate in Nabire, a small city on the north coast of the island on the Pacific Ocean to start a new theological school on a senior high level. I doubted that I had what it took to undertake such a tremendous job, but the brethren were insistent that they wanted me to do it.

However, the house that the Mission intended to rent for us was still under construction, and it would be several months before it was ready. There was no place for us to live in Nabire. In the meantime, we went to Sentani, where we settled temporarily and began a teaching ministry in the Ruland Lesnussa Bible School in Abepura.

February 14, 1979: The children left today to go to school in Malaysia. There was a rather large group of twenty students. Last night, the MAF people organized a farewell for them with films, ice cream and other delicacies. In the last few years, the trip has become much easier. The Indonesian airline flies with jets to Jakarta. The use of jets means that the trip takes seven hours, instead of eleven as before. The children were in an exuberant mood. Mitch behaved in a manly way, but Viviane found it difficult to say good-bye and left with many tears. It is difficult to put into words what this means for the parents. Fortunately, we had a lot of work waiting for us when we returned from the airport.

We have to move out of the vacation house where we have lived since we arrived because there are guests coming tomorrow who had already signed up for the house months ahead of time. For the weekend, we can move into the vacation house of another Mission society, but then we are facing the same problem again. We heard that there is a small house that will become available and won't be needed until June. We will look into that. We want to be able to settle somewhere and unpack our suitcases. The Mission had signed a contract with a contractor for a house in Abepura. This is a common practice. A house might still be under construction when someone signs up to rent it for a four-year period, and the rent is paid in advance. After the contractor had accepted the money from the Mission and spent it on building material, he came to tell our field chairman that the rent was too low and that he wanted seventy-three percent more! It may take months before this matter is settled satisfactorily, if ever. This is the reason that we want to rent a house in Sentani.

February 15: "What do you have there, sir?" asked the man who sat next to me in the communal taxi which I had boarded for my trip back from Abepura to Sentani. I showed him the Tupperware with breadfruit which the director of the Bible school had given to me. The other passengers, as well as the taxi driver, now joined the conversation. "That looks delicious," they all agreed. "You mind if we try a little piece?" An Indonesian taxi is not a private means of transportation, and a white man's luggage is not his private property either. So the lid was taken off, and more than half of the pungent smelling, piquant tasting tropical fruit was distributed. This loosened everyone's tongue.

"Are you from America?"

"No, I am Dutch," I replied.

The reaction was very enthusiastic.

"Many of our people live in Holland," the taxi driver said. "I myself come originally from the island of Ambon."

"I know there are a lot of Ambonese in the Netherlands," I said, thinking of the recent news I had heard over the radio about a group of Ambonese who had hijacked a train. I didn't think it wise to bring up that subject.

The conversation rolled along happily. I knew that most Ambonese consider themselves to be Christians. According to the law in Indonesia, one is not allowed to ask about someone's beliefs in public because it can be construed as an attempt to proselytize. The Muslims especially are very sensitive on

THE LORD'S DOING

this point. If people ask someone a question, he may give the inquirer answers. The fact that our witness has to be more in our conduct than in our words is in itself not a bad thing. The law against proselytizing does not hinder the progress of the gospel in practice. I trust that my breadfruit distribution did, in a way, witness for me.

The immediate result of the fruit was that I had no trouble convincing the driver that I wanted to be let out on top of the hill, instead of at the bottom. Most taxi drivers don't like to drive up the bad road, which means that often I have to walk the one mile to our house in the hot tropical sun. The fact that I didn't have to do that now was certainly worth a few pieces of breadfruit.

March 9: Since we had been asked to build and start a theological school in Nabire, I asked for permission to make a trip to look the place over. Janine and I left Sentani early this morning for the two-and-a-half-hour flight from the coast, via the mountains, and back to the coast some 400 miles farther west. To my great joy, we made a landing in Enarotali, and from a distance we could see Kebo, the place that had been our home for thirteen years.

We had not been in Nabire for five years and could hardly recognize the place. Where there used to be a small path through the jungle, we found a blacktop road. The little village with houses on stilts had disappeared completely. All the houses were concrete structures. The migration of Kapauku people to the coast had taken on enormous proportions, and we were greeted enthusiastically by a host of friends we knew from the Wissel Lakes. The tribal church organized a special meeting to welcome us, and I was asked to preach that same afternoon.

March 10: Eventually, we will have to build a house here, but that may take a while; we anticipate that we will have to rent for at least one year.

March 11: I was asked to preach in the Indonesian-speaking church this morning. After the service, we had a short meeting to discuss plans for three different retreats the church wants to organize for the months of June and July—a children's camp, a youth retreat and a ladies' retreat. Janine and I have been asked to speak. In the afternoon I met with the school board for the school-to-be to discuss plans for the opening. There was tremendous enthusiasm, which indicates that we are definitely wanted here. We feel that we should take advantage of the current tide of confidence and approval.

March 12: We flew from Nabire to Kebo. It gave us a strange feeling to land there again after an absence of three years. What a happy reunion we had with a large group of friends. Yet, this visit was a confirmation of what we knew already, that our work in Kebo was finished. We have now closed the door on that chapter of our lives. It is time to make a new beginning.

May 25: Today actually started a new phase in our missionary career. At 6 o'clock this morning, we left Sentani for Nabire. We flew in a twin-engine plane with lots of space for cargo, so that we were able to take our newly acquired piano, our motorbikes and all our other outfit with us. I had discovered a piano in the corner of the M.K. school gym. The students of last year had painted it in the colors of the United States flag to celebrate the bicentennial and then stored it. I offered the mission $40 for it, and so it became mine. It needs a lot of repair work, but that will give me something to do in my spare hours in the months to come.

The Heglunds, Alliance missionaries in Nabire, welcomed us. For the first week, we will live in the house of a missionary couple of another organization who are on vacation. That week will give us time to clean the apartment we are going to rent. The apartment is rather small which means that we will be crowded when Mitch and Viviane come home on vacation, but it will be workable. We will have to put screens in front of the windows to keep mosquitoes out, and since there is no running water, we will have to rig up some fifty-five-gallon drums.

What a beautiful place Nabire is. Only a few steps away is the measureless Pacific Ocean with its deep blue water, and behind us rise the hazy blue mountains and the luxuriant jungle. If only it were ten or twenty degrees cooler, it would be a utopia. The heat and humidity are stifling.

July 20: On our way back from our yearly mission's conference, which was this year held in Sentani, we ran into problems. With another missionary family, we left Sentani in a twin-engine airplane about 2 p.m. which is late for flying in Irian Jaya. Our destination was Nabire.

About half an hour out of Nabire, we ran into very bad weather, and soon we were surrounded by thunderstorms. The pilot had to climb to an altitude of about 17,500 feet, which was a very unpleasant experience since no one except the pilot had oxygen. We endeavored to reach some alternate landing places, but the mountain passes were all closed. Finally, the pilot decided to return to Sentani, but since we began to run low on fuel, we had to land on an airstrip that was actually too short for this kind of plane. Since it was a choice between trying to land in a riverbed or on the short airfield, the latter seemed to be the safer. However, the field had been soaked by a heavy tropical downpour only minutes before we landed.

Upon touchdown, the brakes did not do any good to stop the plane. We skidded over the wet grass like skaters on ice, went off the end of the airstrip, through the fence and into a soggy cow pasture. Miraculously, nobody sustained any injuries; only the airplane suffered a damaged nose wheel. We escaped with only some fright. Actually, we as passengers knew less what was going on than every other missionary on the island. The pilot had reported to his home base about the trouble he was facing. Several missionaries, who had overheard the transmissions on their base radios, were following our adventures and had begun praying for our safety. The missionaries on the station whose airfield we had used as a shuffleboard and whose fence we had ruined received us very warmly.

July 21: A plane with MAF experts from Sentani arrived. They decided that the plane could be flown out and repaired in their hangar. Another plane was sent to take us back to Nabire, where we arrived safely without any further incidents.

September 2: Today was our first day of school. I began with a short sermon from Daniel chapter 1; then I proceeded to collect tuition money from the students. Not all the students have arrived yet. Some are still waiting for plane connections. The official opening of the school will be next week when the district superintendent returns from his trip to the interior of the island.

I remember during our farewell from the First Alliance Church in Atlanta saying jokingly: "I know what will happen when we arrive in Nabire; the district superintendent of the area will take me into the jungle and say, 'Here it is. Go ahead and begin with your school!' " Those words turned out to be quite prophetic, for when we arrived in Nabire that is almost exactly what happened. Rev. Frans Titahelew, the district superintendent of the Gospel Tabernacle Church of Irian Jaya (the official name of the church established by The Christian and Missionary Alliance in Indonesia), took me by bike into the jungle and then another twenty minutes by foot. We arrived at a place where the undergrowth had been somewhat cleared off.

"Here we can have about sixty acres," Frans said.

The trees were beautiful, but most of them would have to be felled to make room for the campus, and there was no road into this place where a truck could bring building materials. We prayed, however, and asked the Lord to guide us if this was the place He had in mind for us. Shortly after this first trip, we found out that the plot we had our eyes on was no no-man's land, but that the Indonesian military had a claim on it. Since they had guns, and we were unarmed, we decided not to argue with them.

This left us without a prospect of terrain on which to build. Various options were investigated, and with every single one we came to a dead end. The Bethesda Church, a large congregation of racially mixed Alliance believers in Nabire, had a place of just two or three acres behind their church building in town. They offered it to us for a dormitory. The church could then be used during the week for a classroom. We settled for that, and in August of 1979 a group of about twenty-five eager students began their studies in the church building.

Before anything could be built on the lot behind the church, Frans Titahelew came around again.

"I found a beautiful place for your school," he said excitedly.

"Sir," I answered, "this is the fifth beautiful place you are recommending to me. Let's forget about it, and stay where we are."

"You could at least go and have a look, couldn't you?" he replied.

I gave in, and that afternoon we went to look at an abandoned tapioca plantation.

A few years earlier, the United Nations representatives in Irian Jaya had suggested that Nabire could profit from a factory where tapioca starch would be produced. So a large area of jungle had been cleared off and planted with tapioca, and a building had been erected to process the roots. After some months of successful operation, the enterprise was handed over to the local population who managed to run it into the ground in just a few months. When the director of the factory took the money that was in the cash box and fled to Java, the factory was closed down.

The local government was quite embarrassed about the whole affair and tried to cover up the scandal. Frans, who was a member of the city council, knew about it, and asked if part of the plantation could be given to the church for the opening of a theological school. When I saw the place, I knew immediately that this was the most ideal spot we could imagine. A rather large river flowed along the property, the land had been cleared, the factory building could be used as a temporary dormitory and classroom, and the land would be given to us free of charge. If this wasn't the Lord's doing!

The only thing needed was to have the land surveyed. This had to be done by the Department of Agriculture. Frans made the arrangements for the survey to take place one week after we decided to accept the government's gift. That week came and went without a survey being carried out. The following week was designated for the purpose. That one also passed without any activity. The next week, the department would have come if the equipment needed for the survey had not been taken to a local exhibition. And so it went.

One morning, during the last class hour of the day, all of a sudden I had a flash of illumination. This was

Satan's effort to thwart our plans. I told the students to stop what they were doing, explained to them what had dawned upon me, and I asked them to pray.

"Lord, if this is the piece of land You want us to have, please let it be surveyed. If not, show us another piece."

Before the class was dismissed, the district superintendent came with word that the Department of Agriculture promised to come and do the survey the next morning.

All the students gathered at the tapioca plantation at 7.30 a.m., but not one of the survey crew showed up. After waiting about one hour, we repeated our prayer meeting of the day before. One of our students had a license to ride a motorbike, so I sent him to town with my motorbike to find out what was keeping the crew from coming. We prayed while he was gone. Half an hour later, he came back with the main surveyor, a fat man who almost flattened the tire on my bike. He was very apologetic, but I forget what his excuses were. Two more trips into town brought the rest of the survey crew. The students cleared a path around the property, and within a few hours the thirteen acres were ours.

The mandate to open a new theological school in Nabire involved everything imaginable: property had to be secured, buildings were to be erected, students accepted, teachers contracted, a curriculum planned, books found, finances procured. The church was very generous in giving me a free hand to plan as I saw fit, but they did not have a dime to back up their plans. Their general philosophy, however, was that all missionaries were millionaires, and if they weren't, their personal friends were millionaires who would open the floodgates upon request. But fund-raising had never been my strong point.

In our periodic prayer letters, we wrote about the new ministry we were entering into, and although we did not openly solicit funds, it was understood that people could contribute if they wanted to. One of our letters reached a friend in Holland whose husband worked at the E.O., a Dutch Christian radio and TV station. They talked it over and undertook to make our needs known to their organization. The E.O. decided to air a program about us and our ministry and to ask people to send contributions. We didn't learn about this until the project was completed; and we received a letter from Holland saying that the E.O. would send us $10,000 for the building of our theological school. Receiving this letter was a deeply emotional experience, a confirmation that we were doing what the Lord wanted us to do.

Clive Alexander was a young man from New Zealand, who represented World Vision International (WVI) in Irian Jaya. I had heard about his organization, but didn't know exactly what their ministry involved apart from a vague notion that they donated goats to people in villages. Clive told me that he was very interested in what we planned to do in Nabire. He wanted to know how much money we would need in the next five years and suggested that I give him a proposed budget which he could present to his organization.

A few weeks later, word came back from WVI's headquarters that they would underwrite fifty percent of our budget. They would appreciate, though, if we could incorporate a project that would benefit the school and that had the character of a development plan. They suggested that we raise cattle, but we would need many more acres of grazing land if we were to raise cattle. Therefore, we decided to start a chicken farm which would require much less space.

We ordered one-day-old chicks from Surabaya, one of the main cities in Indonesia. We visualized the chicks growing into healthy laying hens. World Vision paid all the expenses for the project that became known as our Lay Training Institute! The chickens became an important part of our theological school, and the sale of eggs to local restaurants provided for over half of the money needed to run the school, keeping tuition down to a manageable level.

Janine and I moved to the tapioca plantation in March 1980, as soon as the house we had contracted to be built was finished. Part of the abandoned Tapioca Starch Factory, which still had all its machinery in it, was converted into dormitories for our married students, with a few rooms for the single fellows and one room for a classroom. This room had a low roof of corrugated iron and no ceiling. After the tropical sun had beaten on it for a few hours, I had the impression that my brain would melt. By noon the heat was unbearable. But we used this classroom for almost two years until the campus was sufficiently developed to move into our own facilities.

The Nabire District decided that the school should be named for the first Alliance missionary who had opened the Wissel Lakes for the gospel—Walter Post. But Walter Post refused to let his name stand. Shortly afterward, however, he passed away, and the church immediately named the school The Walter Post Theological School. I don't know if Walter Post's life was shortened by this act of humility, but I decided that if ever someone asked me to lend my name to an institution, I would not refuse.

The development of the campus was another challenge; I had never before faced such a project. I discussed with the district committee my plans for the buildings, and they gave me a free hand to do as I pleased. I drew up rough sketches for a two-story dormitory with twenty-four rooms for married students and singles, a residence for the director of the school, two buildings for classrooms, an office, a library and a chapel. These sketches were taken to a local contractor whose architect transformed them into beautiful blueprints. I had never before undertaken such a project, and it wasn't until after the buildings were finished that I recognized how carefully the Lord had supervised my scribbles.

Some of the buildings were innovative, at least for Irian Jaya. A two-story dormitory was unheard of, but constructing the building in that way saved us a substantial amount of money on roofing material. The classrooms were open-sided. Unwittingly, I placed them in such a way that the cooler wind from the ocean would make it possible to teach and study a whole morning without any brains melting.

What we didn't realize when the tapioca plantation was given to us was that it had a hidden treasure. For the initial clearing of the land, some huge ironwood trees had been felled, and the trunks were still lying on our property. Some must have been over 100 feet tall with a diameter of about six feet. The Alliance in Irian Jaya had bought a portable sawmill. This saw could be mounted on the trees and would slice them up in whatever size of timber was desired.

Otis Hussey, one of the schoolteachers at the M.K. school in Sentani, who was a former lumberjack, offered to come and help cut the wood for us. He and his wife, Carmelita, spent several of their vacations with us in Nabire. Otis would work from early morning till late in the afternoon in the tropical sun, providing us with hundreds of cubic feet of lumber. We sold this lumber to the contractor, and he then deducted this from the building contract. In this way, the Lord helped us to cut our expenses considerably.

Ironwood makes beautiful and durable building material. When dry, it becomes so hard that one cannot drive a nail into it without drilling first. In a land where the termites outnumber the humans by the millions, such lumber ensures a safe building.

14

A Fiery Fence and DDT

August 21, 1980: Our fellow missionaries, the Heglunds, should have gone on furlough in July of this year, but they couldn't leave Indonesia without a special letter from one of the government departments in Jakarta on the basis of which an exit permit would be issued. This letter had been delayed for six weeks. Finally, word came over the radio today that the letter had arrived. These kinds of frustrating delays are typical of life in this country. Now, they can leave next week.

Our MAF pilot had problems of a different kind. The fuel tank of his airplane sprung a leak. He installed a new tank that promptly sprung a leak also. His radio also stopped functioning. It turned out that the culprit was a rat that had gnawed through the wires. The rat died in the process and was easily located because of the smell it emitted.

August 23: A rat again cut through the same wires of the pilot's plane radio. It cannot have been the same rat, of course! The pilot came up with a foolproof solution—a cat now spends the night in the airplane.

September 21: We are spending this weekend in the city of Wamena, in the Baliem Valley. Janine and I are both members of the committee for the preparation of next year's conference. We have to put together the programs and ordered the food. This morning I was asked to preach in the Indonesian-speaking church in the city. We met with Mr. and Mrs. Sumilat, who served with us in the Kebo Bible School several years back. They are now working with an American help organization called Mustard Seed. I have hinted to them that, if they ever felt called that way, we would give them a warm welcome in Nabire. Mr. Sumilat would be the ideal director for our Bible school in Nabire.

September 22: Back in Nabire. The work on the dormitory has not started yet. The contractor has cement now, but no work crew. He is trying to recruit people from Jayapura who are supposed to arrive on the next boat. This boat should have arrived two weeks ago, but is now anchored in Biak with engine trouble. The carpenter who should be working on our school benches has not shown his face yet. And our generator has burned out because of a short circuit. We sent it to Jayapura to be rewound.

September 24: The boat's arrival today gives us hope that the work on the dormitory will start soon.

September 29: Finally, the architect came today with some workmen to prepare the ground for the building of the dormitory. The old shed that was still on our property, as a reminder of the construction of our house, was taken apart and reerected at the new building site. One of the contractor's carpenters declared himself willing to make benches for the school. Some light is shining at the end of the tunnel.

October 1, 1981: I went to see the contractor yesterday; he officially handed me the keys for the school building and the dormitory without one word of apology for the fact that it took more than a year to finish the project. This is the day we have anticipated for over two years. Some things are still not quite finished, but the buildings are ready for occupancy. Mr. Sumilat, who is now the director of the school, will oversee the moving of the students into the dormitory, and I am in charge of the moving into the classrooms. The temporary shelters we had built for the students in the tapioca factory will have to be torn down, and the pile of plywood and ironwood two-by-fours will have to be stacked somewhere for later use. The students will have to move all their belongings to their new rooms, and the benches, made from ironwood (and heavy as lead), will have to be moved to the new classrooms. Then, everything will have to be cleaned before it can be installed in the new facilities. This will take at least two days.

The classrooms have open sides, and every little waft of wind can pass through. We are grateful for the marked cooling effect.

October 5: I had just finished my class when Janine sent me a note saying that the MAF pilot from Nabire, Tom Vanderbroek, had had a plane accident. No details were known. Janine and I left immediately for the MAF base in town to be with Tom's wife, Diane. We learned that radio contact had been lost with the plane soon after it took off from Hitadipa. Another aircraft that was nearby flew over the area and saw the wreck in the vicinity of one of the villages nearby. It was not known whether there were any survivors. I did something absolutely irrational: I prayed with Diane and thanked the Lord that He had allowed this to happen. It is a wonder that Diane didn't slap my face, but the urge to pray this prayer simply overwhelmed me. We stayed with her for several hours.

Later in the morning, we heard that some people from the village had gone to tell the Cuttses that the pilot and two passengers were still alive, but unconscious. They made a makeshift stretcher and carried the three victims to the Cutts' residence. Two doctors were flown in by helicopter. Poor Diane didn't hear until later that there was hope that her husband would survive.

October 12: Tom Vanderbroek is in a mission hospital in the mountains. He was in a coma for three or four days, and begins to come to slowly. He probably suffered brain damage. He speaks a little, but most of what he says makes no sense. We receive daily progress reports. Diane, who is pregnant and has two small children, is at his side. One of the doctors has performed surgery on him. He has cuts and bruises and a broken wrist. By the looks of the pictures of the airplane wreck, it is a sheer miracle that he came out alive.

October 29: This morning, a telex from our daughter Ruthy and her husband was read to us over the radio: "Congratulations to the future grandparents." Janine and I performed a little dance in our living room. We will not be able to witness the birth of our first grandchild, but we hope to go on furlough a few months after the birth.

November 6: On our way to Tembagapura, we landed in Enarotali, where we found a large concentration of Indonesian military. We had to show our travel passes (one doesn't travel anywhere in Irian Jaya without permission) and received our stamped papers back. A group of rebels has been spotted in the Enarotali area. Most of the local people don't want to have anything to do with them. They represent a strange mixture of nationalism, a desire for independence from the Indonesian government in Jakarta and a materialistic messianic movement (cargo cult). Numerically they are not very significant, but they do generate a lot of noise and make all kinds of impossible and unrealistic promises to the people in the villages.

November 9: On our return trip from Tembagapura, we landed in Kebo, where Tom Vanderbroek joined us. He was deeply moved when he saw us and hugged us warmly. He looks well, but has to wear some kind of abdominal belt because he has a couple of broken ribs and a cracked vertebra. His speech is rather slow, and he is not anymore the funny, jovial fellow we used to know.

December 24: Christmas Eve was desecrated by a fight in the village next to our house. Less than 300 feet from our house, there are several little houses belonging to people from the Biak tribe. I heard loud wails coming from that direction and decided to go and see what was going on. It sounded as if someone had died. It turned out to be a drunken man who was beating his wife. He had put himself in the spirit of Christmas with an excessive amount of alcohol.

A cluster of people came tumbling out of the ramshackle huts when I approached. Some of the men tried to separate the man from his wife, but he resolutely dragged her behind him. They tried persuasion, shouting: "Please, Uncle, don't! Let her go!" To no avail! In reply, the drunk kicked and swung his arms wildly around him to keep people at a distance. I barely escaped a direct hit. I shouted: "You should be ashamed to do this on Christmas Eve." The miracle happened; everyone became silent, and the man let go of his wife. She disappeared immediately. I didn't understand myself what had happened. It surely was the Lord.

In July 1984, our youngest daughter Viviane was going to marry Matt Miner. Our financial condition was a little better than it had been a few years earlier, but we didn't think we could afford for both of us to attend the wedding. So it was decided that Janine would go, and I would stay in Nabire. This was too much for Viviane to take, so she mobilized her own prayer warriors to storm the gates of heaven.

One day she found an anonymous letter in her mailbox which read: "We believe that every father should be able to attend his daughter's wedding," with a substantial gift to back up this creed. So, because of the Lord's provision, we both attended the wedding.

Our Lay Training Institute had been a source of constant pride and care thus far. I almost came to the point that I felt tempted to regard the chickens as more important than our students. After all, they laid the eggs that kept the school going. In every prayer letter, our chickens were mentioned. So, although we were rather amused, we were not too amazed when our friend, Frank Nagle, the faithful night watchman on the radio station WRAF of Toccoa Falls College, greeted us at the weekly prayer meeting, with the words: "John, how are your chickens? I am praying for them."

"Thanks, Frank," I said. "They were fine when we left."

We chuckled somewhat when Frank loudly and warmly prayed for our chickens during that prayer meeting, thinking that it was nice, and it certainly wouldn't do any harm.

After Viviane and Matt's wedding, when we arrived back in Nabire, we were met at the plane by Mr. Sumilat. His first words were: "There has been a sickness among the chickens in town. Some people have lost all they had." My first question, of course, was, "How about the school chickens?" "Something strange happened," he said. "One morning three chickens died, and then the sickness stopped." We asked when this had happened. "It was Thursday morning." There is a time difference of fourteen hours between Irian Jaya and the east coast of the United States. Thursday morning in Nabire was Wednesday evening in Toccoa.

When Frank prayed, our chickens were dying. But the Lord heard and stopped the sickness right then and there. If God does this for a bunch of chickens, what will He do for us?

We thought of Jesus' words: "Look at the birds of the air; they do not sow or reap or store away in barns, and yet your heavenly Father feeds them. Are you not much more valuable than they?" (Matthew 6:26). And, "Are not two sparrows sold for a penny? Yet not one of them will fall to the ground apart from the will of your Father. And even the very hairs of your head are all numbered. So don't be afraid; you are worth more than many sparrows" (10:29-31).

The Lord also heard our prayers for the students, but we had to learn how to pray for them. Because of the constant threat of malaria, we gave out medicine on a weekly basis. This would assure that nobody would get sick, or so we thought. But our students did get deathly sick with malaria. It was pitiful to see them sitting in class, all of a sudden beginning to shiver with uncontrollable shakes, followed immediately by a rise in temperature to 104°F or more. The sickness could get into the brain and endanger the person's life. We insisted, therefore, that the students would come and see us immediately upon the first sign of malaria.

Josef Yelemaken's wife was the cutest girl in school. She was about sixteen. Every day she would pass my office with a load of pots and pans on her way to the river to do her dishes. I could hear the clicking and rattling coming from a distance. She did not like the malaria prophylaxis we gave out because the pills were too bitter. So she didn't take them. We didn't know this, of course. We also didn't know that she was pregnant, and when she came down with an apparent attack of malaria and received a treatment, she started having a miscarriage. She was taken to the local hospital where the doctor thought he might have to perform an operation. He asked for volunteers to give blood in case it was needed. Some of us, who had the same blood type, were waiting at the hospital when we were told that no operation was needed. She had delivered a premature dead baby.

Josef was distraught when he came to tell me this. His wife seemed to be in stable condition, so I went home. In the afternoon, Josef came running to our house, out of breath. He had run the two miles from the hospital through a heavy tropical downpour. His wife wasn't doing well. She had been taken to the ward, then all of a sudden, her eyes turned back in her head. We made him a pot of tea and gave him a sandwich; he hadn't eaten anything the whole day. Then I took him back to the hospital on the back of my motorbike.

When we arrived, we learned that his wife had died a few minutes earlier in an apparent attack of malaria. I watched as Josef knelt beside the body of his young wife and howled like a wounded animal. It was a heartrending scene, and my sympathy went out to him. I knew to do nothing better than put my arms around him and pray with him.

Barely three weeks later, we went back to the hospital to see another student's wife who had been admitted two days earlier. She had been improving, but when we arrived, we heard that she had passed away twenty minutes earlier in an attack of cerebral malaria. Her husband sat on the concrete floor next to her bed and cried softly. Twice in one month we passed through the same trauma.

During the first few years of the school's existence, we had eight of our students or members of their families die as a result of malaria. Was the Lord still among us? Was this a place where our students came to study the Word of God, or did they come here to die? We felt we were under severe attack by the enemy.

The hardest case was the death of the eight-year-old daughter of Amos Tenouye. It seemed to be the straw that broke the camel's back. As I sat in the classroom where the small coffin had been placed on a table for the memorial service, I was rebellious and felt as if I had lost one of my own children. I prayed and confessed my sin before the Lord. I recognized that He had a right to call to Himself whomever He wanted and whenever He wanted, but my heart rebelled against this seemingly senseless death. Yet, when I prayed, I said to the Lord that I believed He was in control. I asked Him to erect a fiery fence around the property of the school where death would not be allowed to enter. This prayer request was passed on to our home constituency via our periodic prayer letters. And the Lord heard us. This little girl was the last one to die, and for several years no one died on our campus as a result of malaria.

Some years later, our prayer vigil must have slackened, and we had another fatality. The students understood that, like the fences that are put around their sweet potato gardens to keep the pigs out, this fence

A FIERY FENCE AND DDT

also had to be mended from time to time to keep out the enemy.

One night, Solaiman came to wake me up. His wife was dying, he said. I took my flashlight and followed him to the school dormitory. I didn't think she was dying, but she was quite sick with diarrhea and vomiting. It looked like some kind of food poisoning, so I questioned the family about what they had eaten the day before. "Fish," was the answer. Nabire, lying on the shore of the Pacific Ocean, has good fish at the market, but with the fish exposed to the tropical heat and no ice to keep it fresh, it has to be eaten within a few hours. It seemed a logical conclusion to blame the fish, especially since some other family members showed similar symptoms. I prayed for them all, gave them some medication and went back to bed.

The next day was Sunday. Janine and I got ready to go to the Indonesian church in town where I was to preach. One of the students caught up to me and handed me a plastic bag with something that looked like flour.

"There is something strange about this fish we ate. We bought a large fish at the market, and since it was too big for one family we shared it with another group. None of the people who ate the other piece got sick, but we all did. Maybe it wasn't the fish that was bad but this flour we used on it before we fried it."

I stuck my finger in the white powder, and sniffed it; this wasn't flour—it was DDT.

I had no idea what to do, so I went to our two-way radio to try to contact one of our doctors. A lady doctor from New Zealand answered my call and told me in no uncertain terms that there was no antidote for

DDT. "Let's just hope that your patients threw up a lot," she said. This was not very comforting. I decided to make another trip to the dormitory before going to church. As I was walking along the path, the Lord reminded me of the words in Mark's Gospel:

> These signs will accompany those who believe: In my name they will drive out demons; they will speak in new tongues; they will pick up snakes with their hands; and when they drink deadly poison, it will not hurt them at all; they will place their hands on sick people, and they will get well. (16:17-18)

"Lord," I prayed, "let this apply to people who have swallowed DDT also." I prayed once more with each of the sick students, and I reminded the Lord of His promise. Then Janine and I left to go to church. I asked the people in the church to pray. When I told them the story, there were cries of "Oh, no!" On our way back home, the Lord tested my faith, and I found myself making a mental calculation to decide how much wood we would need for the coffins we would have to make on Monday morning to bury those who had died. I was sure there would be fatalities.

Once at home, my first trip was to the dormitory. The place was strangely quiet, and I saw no trace of my patients. Finally, I located one student.

"Where are all the sick people?" I asked.

"Nobody is sick anymore," was the answer. "After you prayed, they got up and went to the river to take a bath, and I haven't seen them back yet." Never in my life had the Lord answered my prayers in such a dramatic way.

15

Turning Points

Most of our students belonged to the mountain tribes that inhabit the interior of the island. Several of them whom we knew quite well had graduated from the Bible school in Kebo, and they wanted to take advantage of this opportunity for further study. In the course of the years, we attracted some people from the tribes that live along the north coast and also a few who came from other Indonesian islands, people with racial features quite different from the Papuans of Irian Jaya.

One of these students was a young man by the name of Bob. Bob applied at the very beginning for the first semester. A bright and pleasant fellow, he had worked as an agent for a domestic Indonesian airline on one of the islands off the coast. Bob seemed to be a real asset to the school, and we received him with open arms. After a few months, rumors began to fly around about him. He had registered as a single student, but the gossip was that he was actually married and had a child. When a letter arrived in our mailbox, addressed to Bob and with a sender shown as Mrs. Bob _____, I decided to call him into my office.

Bob belonged to the same tribe and originated from the same island as the district superintendent of the Nabire district. It didn't take me long to discover that he knew Bob's story in detail but chose not to inform me for fear that Bob would be placed on discipline. Blood, after all, is thicker than water, and scandals are covered up within the family, especially where foreigners are concerned.

Now, Bob was sitting in front of me, his head sunken low on his chest.

"What happened, Bob?" I asked as kindly as I could. A deep sigh was the answer. Finally, the story came out, each fragment interrupted by deep sighs.

Before he came to Nabire, he had befriended a girl on the island where he worked and had gotten her pregnant. The theological school in Nabire seemed a safe place to hide from the scandal, so Bob enrolled. The Lord's call had nothing to do with it. The girl's parents, however, were not accepting the fact that their daughter was expecting a baby and that the father had fled the scene. So they contacted Bob's parents who called their son home during Christmas vacation. Not knowing what had happened, and since it seemed logical that he wanted to see his family, I had given him permission to go home.

Both sets of parents were adamant that the couple get married. Therefore, they did exchange wedding vows just a few days before the baby was born. As all this came out piecemeal, Bob let out his last sigh and declared that he felt much better. My heart went out to this young man. We had a long talk and prayed together. I told him that the school and the church would require that he be put on discipline for a one-year period, but that we would be happy to consider taking him back the following year. I promised that I would try to find him a job and suggested that he call his wife and little son to come to Nabire so they could live together as a family.

MAF in Nabire was happy to hire Bob. He became such a valuable agent that they didn't want to let him go at the end of his disciplinary time. But Bob wanted to continue his study to serve the Lord and not to run away from Him. So MAF allowed him to work part-time. This he did for the rest of his schooling. After graduation, MAF hired him back, and this has become his life ministry. Looking back upon his experiences, Bob told me once that the hour he spent in my office was the best thing that ever happened to him. It was the turning point of his life.

We were able to go home for the wedding of one of our children. Before leaving Nabire, we made plans so that upon our return we could not only resume school without delay, but also would be able to take in a second class of students. The first year, we had had the help of a young college graduate of the Jaffray Theological School in Ujung Pandang, Indonesia. Jance Tuhumuri had told us, though, that he wanted to go back to school for further study. We had asked the president of the Irian Jaya church to get us a replacement for him. He promised to have a substitute. One classroom was under construction, but we would need a second classroom to accommodate the second group. This was contracted out, as were the benches needed for the second class.

When we returned to Nabire after a wonderful trip home, our plane landed in a tropical downpour. As soon as we arrived at the campus, it was obvious what had happened—nothing. Some things had gone according to schedule: Jance Tuhumuri had left, but there was no replacement. The new students had all arrived, but there was no second classroom building. The contractor had run out of cement. The carpenter had forgotten all about the benches I had ordered. I felt like throwing in the towel. There would be about seventy class hours to teach, and the only teachers available were Janine and me, leaving us with an unmanageable load of thirty-five teaching hours a week. We had one classroom for two classes and benches enough to seat only half of the students. The next morning I got up early to have my devotions, and the Lord guided me to a passage of Scripture I had not intended to read:

> The whole Israelite community set out from the Desert of Sin, traveling from place to place as the LORD commanded. They camped at Rephidim, but there was no water for the people to drink. So they quarreled with Moses and said, "Give us water to drink."
>
> Moses replied, "Why do you quarrel with me? Why do you put the LORD to the test?"
>
> But the people were thirsty for water there, and they grumbled against Moses. They said,

"Why did you bring us up out of Egypt to make us and our children and livestock die of thirst?"

Then Moses cried out to the LORD, "What am I to do with these people? They are almost ready to stone me."

The LORD answered Moses, "Walk on ahead of the people. Take with you some of the elders of Israel and take in your hand the staff with which you struck the Nile, and go. I will stand there before you by the rock at Horeb. Strike the rock, and water will come out of it for the people to drink." So Moses did this in the sight of the elders of Israel. And he called the place Massah and Meribah because the Israelites quarreled and because they tested the LORD saying, "Is the LORD among us or not?" (Exodus 17:1-7)

It struck me that the Israelites found themselves in circumstances even more desperate than mine, not because of their disobedience, but because they had obeyed the command of the Lord. I had no doubt in my mind that the Lord wanted us in Nabire. He had given us enough assurances on that point. It seemed that Israel's problem was a lack of water. This turned out to be wrong; there was water in the rock, but no one knew that apart from God. The issue was not "Is there water?" but "Is the LORD among us or not?" Looking at our problems in Nabire from that perspective did not immediately suggest solutions, but it helped to set things in perspective. I prayed and thanked the Lord for what He was going to do.

The students arrived for their first day of school which started with a chapel service followed by campus cleanup. The ever-hungry jungle had tried to reclaim some of our campus during the few months' vacation. For my chapel talk I read the above portion of Scripture and commented on the thought it had evoked in me. I said: "I have no idea what the Lord is going to do for us, but I believe we will see Him work things out." Then the students got their machetes and went to work.

When I walked outside, I bumped into Jerry Supplig, the pastor of the Indonesian church where the school had started. Jerry asked me what I was going to do without the new teacher who had been promised but hadn't shown up. I told him I didn't know. Then he offered himself to teach the next semester in the school. In the Indonesian culture one cannot hug a friend, but I felt like hugging Jerry. He was God's answer to our prayer.

We walked back into the classroom. Then, all of a sudden, I remembered that at the Brussels Bible Institute, where Janine and I had received our training, classes were not separated according to year. The school had been too small to divide up the students. There was a cycle of nine trimesters. A student could enter the course at the beginning of any of those trimesters and would stay till he or she had completed the cycle. Why couldn't we do this in Nabire? We would teach the second-year subjects to both classes together. This would cut the number of class hours in half. Instead of seventy hours there would only be thirty-five to teach. And since we now had a staff of three teachers, there would be a manageable load of about twelve hours per teacher.

Seating was still a problem. Jerry and I were standing in front of the classroom when my eye fell upon some two-by-fours in the back of the room. They were left over from the temporary dormitory rooms we had constructed in the factory. We could place those between the seats on the benches and two students could sit on those, while two others would sit on the bench. For the sake of fairness, it was decided that the students on the benches would trade places with those on the two-by-fours in order to avoid afflicting undue punishment to certain parts of the body. The arrangements were primitive and temporary, but that particular school year stands out in my mind as our finest year ever.

John Gobai didn't understand enough English to be able to fill out the form himself, so he asked me to do it for him. He had received an application for the Congress of Itinerant Evangelists, to be held in Amsterdam, Holland in July of 1983, organized by the Billy Graham Association. The cost for transportation, registration fee and hotel would be his responsibility. I tried to explain to him that he would never be able to come up with that much money, but he insisted that I fill out the form anyway. So I did. He signed it and sent it in. I enclosed a letter to the chairman of the committee, explaining that for John Gobai to attend the congress was a sheer impossibility.

"Even if he sold some of his pigs," I wrote, "he would probably have just enough money to fly to the capital, Jakarta, which is the point from which his trip to Europe would only commence." I added: "But if you would be interested to invite a representative of a Stone-Age tribe, I have a worthy sample for you." I promptly forgot about the application and went back to my daily duties.

By the end of that year, 1982, Janine and I went on furlough, which we spent in Toccoa, Georgia. In the spring of the next year, after I had returned from tour ministry, I received an unexpected phone call from a friend in Atlanta who was the manager of one of the branches of the Day's Inn motel chain. Woody had attended the Sunday school class I taught in Atlanta. He informed me that the Day's Inn Foundation was one of the sponsors of Billy Graham's Congress for Itinerant Evangelists in Amsterdam. He also told me that the organizing committee had received John Gobai's application and that they would pay his way from Irian Jaya as well as his expenses while in the Netherlands. The only problem the committee faced was that they needed an interpreter for John.

My reaction was, "That shouldn't be too difficult. There are a lot of people who speak Indonesian in Holland. After all, Indonesia used to be a Dutch colony." Woody told me that the committee had written to me in Irian Jaya, but since I had not answered them, they concluded that I must be lost somewhere in the jungle. When Woody heard this, he had said: "John Schultz is not lost in the jungle; he is on furlough in the U.S.A."

At this point, I was linked to a party line on the phone, so that Woody, the chairman of the Billy Graham Congress committee and I could discuss the matter together. I repeated my suggestion that somebody in Holland be found who spoke Indonesian. The voice from Amsterdam objected and related how they had run into difficulties during the Berlin Congress when some Aucas from Ecuador had been brought over who found themselves completely lost in such unfamiliar circumstances.

"The Billy Graham Congress would appreciate," he said, "if John Schultz would come to Amsterdam, meet John Gobai at the airport and stay with him throughout the congress." All expenses would be paid for me also. It didn't take me long to determine that this might be the will of the Lord for me! I would, however, have to return to the U.S. a few days before the end of the congress because our son Mitch was planning to get married on July 23. This condition was accepted, and I consented.

Some weeks later, I met a rather travel-weary young man at the airport in Amsterdam and took him to the huge complex where the congress would be held. There we met the chairman of the committee who asked me if I was aware of what had prompted the invitation to bring John and me over. I pleaded ignorance.

"We were deeply moved by your letter, which stated that John was willing to sell his pigs in order to attend this conference," he said. "So we passed the hat among ourselves and, with other contributions, we have come up with enough money to bring over ten evangelists from all over the world who would not have been able to attend because of financial problems." I realized that my letter had been misread, but this wasn't the moment to put things straight. I sensed an avalanche of emotions that would have been impossible to stem. Later, my innocent remark about John's selling off a pig or two was further embellished to the point that he was willing to sell his pig farm (he didn't have a pig farm) in order to attend the congress. As such, the story even appears in Billy Graham's autobiography, *Just as I Am*. So who am I to contradict Billy Graham?

I was amazed to see John's reactions to European civilization. He took most of it in stride. Streetcars, elevators and department stores were no problem for him. What he could not understand was why the sun was still shining brightly at 9 o'clock in the evening. Having grown up at the equator where the sun rises at 6 a.m. and sets at 6 p.m. the year around, this was one of the major miracles for him. He wanted to know how the Dutch managed to keep the sun going that long. I reminded him that I had explained this phenomenon in my classes in the Bible school in Nabire. He remembered but had never believed that I was serious.

My friend Woody, together with another representative of Day's Inns, came over to Amsterdam to meet John Gobai. They wanted to know how they could help him in his work as an evangelist in Irian Jaya. John told them that he would like to be able to show the *Jesus* film. If they could provide him with a copy of the film, he would need a movie projector and a small generator. The two men looked at me and said: "You buy these items for him when you get back to Indonesia, and we will reimburse you."

So when John returned to Irian Jaya, he received the means to do evangelism in a much more effective way than ever before, and most of the meetings and seminars of the congress also proved very beneficial. Also, the fact that he was one of the few men of his tribe who had been to the end of the world and returned to tell about it enhanced his status considerably.

16

"Missionary Stuff"

I had been in the habit of choosing a Scripture verse, or several verses, at the beginning of each year as a guide for the year. For the year 1985 my text was taken from Second Corinthians 12:9-10:

> He said to me, "My grace is sufficient for you, for my power is made perfect in weakness." Therefore I will boast all the more gladly about my weaknesses, so that Christ's power may rest on me. That is why, for Christ's sake, I delight in weaknesses, in insults, in hardships, in persecutions, in difficulties. For when I am weak, then I am strong.

Every morning, I would repeat the verses which I had committed to memory. I soon realized that the Lord was taking my Scripture memorization program much more seriously than I was myself. My boasting in weakness so that Christ's power would rest on me was severely put to the test. All of a sudden, I began to have attacks of malaria in spite of the prophylaxis I was taking faithfully every week. The doctor changed the medication, and for a few weeks the attacks would subside, but then return in full force. Several times, I was prescribed different pills, and the process would repeat itself. I experienced weakness all right, but I found little joy in boasting about it. I promised myself to be more careful in my choice of Scripture verses for the next year, and I longed for this year to come to an end.

Janine and I decided to take a break during the Christmas recess and to spend a few weeks in Sentani. We had vacationed there regularly in years gone by when our children were still in school. One of the couples who were teachers at the school offered us their house since they were going to the mountains for their Christmas vacation. Their black dog, Friday, came with the house, and we enjoyed taking care of him.

It was the last day of the year, and we were fast asleep when Friday's barking woke us up. We didn't think much about it, until the bark changed to a sharp yelp, as if the dog was being attacked. I jumped out of bed and ran to the back porch. There was Friday with a deep gash on his head. Someone had tried to kill the dog with a machete. I gave some first aid and then decided to put Friday in a safer place where the thief, who had obviously planned to break into the house, would not be able to get to him. The lean-to, where the washing machine was situated, had a door that could be locked. So the dog was given shelter there.

We felt, though, that the thief, having seen the light come on and realizing that there were people inside and knowing that they were awake, would give up his efforts. So I went back to bed. After a short time, however, we heard somebody trying to get in through the back door. We got up, turned on all the lights and sat in the living room. Surely the thief would have to abandon his plan. Nobody in his right mind would try to break into a house where the people were sitting waiting for him.

But we were wrong. The thief kept on prowling around the house. We could see him through the window, and he could see us. He pressed his nose against the windowpane and stuck his tongue out at us. *This man must be crazy,* we thought. Later we heard from people of the nearby village that some thieves perform magic on themselves, thinking this makes them invisible. Whatever magic this man had used must have been outdated or something else had gone wrong, because we could see him clearly. He was a young fellow, perhaps seventeen or eighteen years old.

It is not a pleasant experience to sit inside a house with a madman prowling around trying to break in. Unfortunately, the M.K. school had no phone hookup at that time, but there was an intercom between some houses. We were able to wake up one of the teachers of the school who promised to locate the night watchman and send him over. Soon the guard came, armed with bow and arrows, and caught the thief. We could see them, standing on the path in front of the house, arguing fiercely.

I made one of my last mistakes of the year: I went outside and joined the argument. Standing behind the thief and facing the watchman, I said: "This man tried to kill the dog, Friday." This infuriated the guard who had a tender spot in his heart for the animal. He slapped the thief in his face. Needless to say, the thief did not appreciate that. The next events happened so fast that I am not sure about the sequence. The night watchman shouted: "Watch it, he has a knife!" The robber had pulled a dagger out of his belt and was brandishing it.

I was about to make my next mistake. To explain my reasoning of the moment, I have to admit that, not having television on the mission field, it was a novelty to us when we were on furlough. We would enjoy watching interesting programs, among which was professional wrestling. I remembered having seen how one wrestler would immobilize his opponent by wrapping his arm around his chin and pulling his head back in what was professionally called a headlock. I decided to try this on the thief, thinking that I could force him to drop his dagger that way.

I pressed my elbow on his windpipe. What I had not taken into account was that I was fifty-eight years old, and this guy was about eighteen; he was also forty years faster than I was. He stabbed the night watchman in the abdomen and drove his dagger through my elbow. It went so fast that I never felt any pain and, in fact, didn't even know that he had stabbed me until a few minutes later.

The watchman reacted swiftly. In an instant, he put an arrow on his bow and shot the man in the back. He fell to the ground. Still with my arm around his neck, I fell on top of him and hit my head on a stone wall, breaking one of my lenses and splattering the glass around my eye. Blood started filling up my eye, and I thought I was going blind. I decided to concede the fight, pulled my arm from under the robber's head and got up. Then I saw the huge gash in my elbow. I staggered back to the front door. Janine came running out to pull me inside. She put me in a chair, and I promptly blacked out.

When I came to, I was no longer in the chair, but stretched out on a couch, with my head lower than my feet. Dr. Ken Dresser, a medical missionary from Canada, working with TEAM, was bending over me. Dr. Dresser had just returned to Irian Jaya from Canada the day before and had spent the night in the house next to the one we occupied. The Lord had provided this expert medical help even before the emergency occurred!

Limited by the absence of equipment to assess any damage, Dr. Dresser could only judge by the outward appearance. He thought I had been lucky, because, as far as he could determine, no vital parts in my elbow had been touched. The dagger had gone in on top and come out at the bottom. Both holes were sewn up, and several places around my left eye, where the glass had cut, required stitches. The night watchman had not gotten off as well. I heard later from Janine what had happened while I was unconscious.

The watchman had come into the house with his hands clutching his abdomen. "I am injured," he told Janine. When he pulled his hands away, his intestines started spilling out. Janine ordered him to keep his hands on his stomach. When Dr. Dresser came, he had the man transported to the hospital in Jayapura, about twenty-five miles away, for an emergency operation.

To conclude this part of my story, I should report that the operation was successful. When we consider the poor sanitary conditions of hospitals in Irian Jaya and the even poorer medical care, we know that this was a miracle. The watchman and I met several times after this incident and always hugged, as soldiers who have been in the same battle.

Later in the day, I heard what happened to the thief. The police came to the scene and found the man with two arrows in his back, the dagger still in his hand, dead in the ditch into which he had fallen. I found this very hard to accept. My reaction amazed me. I realized it would have been normal for me to consider that this man had received what was coming to him. He had tried to break in and no doubt had intended to murder two people. But suddenly the love of the Lord flooded my soul, and I felt like shedding tears for this man. I could see him standing before the judgment seat of Christ, the dagger with which he had tried to kill still in his hand.

I had had a close brush with death myself. Maybe I had been on my way to heaven when the Lord sent me back to earth. But somehow, this man, who was heading for a lost eternity, was gone. I told the Lord I would have been ready to take his place if he could have been given another chance to hear the gospel. But this was not the way it was to be. I still cannot think of this young man without feeling deep emotions. He has become to me the symbol of what it means to be without Christ in this life.

When the police came, they decided that before they could turn the body of the robber over to his relatives they needed a medical attestation of his death. So they put the body on the back of a pickup truck and sent him to the hospital for a death certificate to be signed by a doctor. In the accompanying letter, they got things mixed up. Somehow my name was substituted for the name of the young man. The doctor who received the letter recognized the mistake and sent the letter to me. The official document, bearing the stamp of the local police commander, stated that the missionary John Schultz died in a stabbing incident on December 31, 1985!

I cannot say, however, that I lived happily ever after. I recovered sufficiently to be able to return to Nabire, but the result of the stabbing remained very painful, and the wound didn't heal properly. After almost five weeks, I made arrangements by radio to go to see a doctor at a hospital in the jungle, about one hour's flying time from Nabire. The evening before my flight, we were having an English church service at the home of one of the missionaries. Suddenly, an artery in my injured arm burst, and blood started spouting through the bandage into the living room, causing some panic in the congregation. I confess that I didn't like it myself.

One of the nurses present applied a tourniquet, which stopped the bleeding, and put me in bed. The next day, I was flown to the hospital. The doctor was a competent general practitioner, but not a surgeon. The idea of opening up my arm did not appeal to him. I stayed for several days, and when finally surgery was performed, it turned out that the dagger had poked two neat holes in a main artery, one at the top and one at the bottom. When one hole closed, the other one would open, thus keeping the arm from healing. Under rather primitive circumstances, this doctor, with the help of an Indonesian colleague, saved my life and my arm. The Lord was in all this. I did not lose my arm to gangrene, as I should have according to some medical opinions, and I regained full strength and use of it.

Several years later, Dr. Peter Nanfelt, then in charge of overseas ministries of the Alliance, reminded me of the fact that my stabbing accident had been one in a series of tragedies that followed in close sequence. It began with the accidental shooting of one of our younger missionaries by the Indonesian military. Then, while I was beginning to recover, the wife of one of our missionaries suddenly passed away while her husband was on a business trip. All these incidents were sent on by telex to the Alliance headquarters in Nyack, N.Y. But the telex machine in the office was down, so the facts were not known at Nanfelt's office. After a few days of telex silence, he instructed his secretary to ask the company if there were any messages that had piled up.

It took a while to convince the clerk on the other end of the phone line that it was legitimate to pass on the information by telephone. He started reading: "John Cutts was shot by the military, John Schultz was injured in a stabbing accident, Mijo Van der Bijl passed away suddenly in Mapnduma." At this point, the telex operator interrupted his reading to ask: "What kind of outfit are you running anyhow?" It must have sounded strange to him when Mr. Nanfelt's secretary told him that this was just "missionary stuff." Actually, it was more an organized attack by God's archenemy on the Lord's work in Irian Jaya.

Linus and Jack wanted another $500 for their work on the chapel, yet they had signed the contract I had drawn up. "Signed" is not the word. Since they were both illiterate, they had drawn a little cross at the bottom of the paper, but at least I had a legal document that would be considered binding. I now realized that a written agreement meant nothing to people who had just come out of the Stone Age and to whom promises and agreements had no value whatsoever. If I refused to pay them, I would lose two good friends who would never give me any help in the future.

When, seven years earlier, I made the first rough sketch of the campus we wanted to develop, the student dormitory was our first priority. It took the crew of skilled Indonesian carpenters almost one whole year to finish that project. The first school building did not fare much better, nor the residence for Rev. and Mrs. Sumilat. We contracted out the second school building to a different contractor, and a smaller dormitory was built by a carpenter from Biak who lived in a village adjacent to our house. By the time we wanted to build the chapel, we had run out of money.

The students, some eighty strong, were now meeting in the largest classroom with space for about twenty-five for the daily chapel services. On Sunday morning we tried to squeeze a crowd of over 100, including several people from the neighboring villages, into that small space for our worship service. So the chapel project became increasingly urgent. Finally, I began to receive some gifts, and I pleaded my cause to the executive committee of the Irian Jaya field. Gradually, we had enough that I thought we could start.

Then I remembered my carpenter friend, Linus, a member of the Kapauku tribe at the Wissel Lakes. Linus could not read or write, but he knew that his measuring tape was five feet long. He also had an unfailing eye for a straight line which he was able to produce with the help of nothing more than a chisel or an ax and a plane. Linus agreed to come to Nabire, and he brought Jack with him as a helper.

I explained to Linus what I wanted and laid out the measurements of the building, being sure that it was squared properly. Then I bought timber from a local sawmill. The term sawmill is misleading. There was no mill, but there were ironwood trees that were felled with a chainsaw and cut up into the desired sizes by the same tool. There was nothing precise in the finished product. The boards and beams had all the indications that the saw had been held by an unsteady hand. But Linus and Jack tackled each piece of timber with their axes, chisels and planes and made them look straight and beautiful.

Within seven months, the sixty-by-thirty-foot building was completed. There were two rooms at the entrance of the building, one for storage and one for prayer and counseling. The side walls were semi-open, with slats of ironwood like half-open blinds, so that the ocean breeze could move freely. A ceiling of one-eighth inch plywood hid the aluminum corrugated roof from the eye, and the wall in back of the podium was also made of plywood. Everything inside was stained with teak oil, and the outside was covered with used oil recovered from the MAF base. I had thirty ironwood benches made, which gave the building a seating capacity of 150. The Alliance logo adorned the wall behind the podium. The whole was beautiful to behold, and all the credit went to these two illiterate young men who had given themselves heart and soul to this project. So I yielded and paid them the extra $500 they wanted. After all, they had saved the school thousands of dollars with their hard work.

The district superintendent officially dedicated the building on October 4, 1987. Thus, the development plan for the campus that had been conceived seven years earlier was finished. And it was obvious that the Lord had had His guiding hand upon it from the beginning.

17

Jack of All Trades

The Lord works in mysterious ways. We knew He had called us to Irian Jaya, and we assumed that our ministry would be with the population of that island. It never crossed our minds that He would bring over people from the other side of the world to Indonesia for the purpose of bringing them to Himself there.

Hans Dekkers was an intelligent young man who had been the pilot of an F16 fighter plane in the Dutch Air Force. Circumstances brought him to Irian Jaya where he joined the flying program of the Catholic Mission. He and with his wife, Rikki, moved to Nabire. They were young, vivacious and outgoing, but religiously neutral. Their reason for doing missionary work had been purely humanitarian.

We met them for the first time in one of the Chinese shops in town and, since Hans and I were both from the same general area in Holland, we began visiting frequently. During one of those visits, Hans mentioned that one of the Alliance missionaries in town had spoken to a friend of his and had presented *The Four Spiritual Laws* to him. The way Hans told the story made me understand that he was saying to me: "Don't you try that on me." Janine and I are not the lapel-grabbing type of evangelists, but we decided to be extra careful in our approach to Hans and Rikki. We prayed regularly that the Lord would open a door to put in a word for Him and that He would lead the conversation in a natural way.

Soon Hans came with a whole series of questions which I tried to answer. Then came the evening when I was able to give the story of my own conversion which seemed to make an impression on him. I asked him if he wanted me to pray with him, but he refused. A few days later, the weather closed in on him after he had landed on one of the small airstrips in the mountains, a place surrounded by native villages, with no white man for miles around. Hans had to spend the night alone in a hut. Before going to bed, he walked back to the airstrip and, in the bright moonlight, he prayed: "Lord, give me what John Schultz has." I felt a mixture of joy and embarrassment when he told me this.

Months went by while we prayed, and Hans resisted. We knew something was moving, though, because he devoured the books by C.S. Lewis I loaned him and commented quite favorably on what he read.

In the fall of 1991, Janine and I were both sent home for emergency health problems. When we returned to Nabire, we heard Hans' story. One afternoon he went to his bedroom, knelt down beside his bed and prayed for Jesus to take over his life. He said that he felt the scales drop from his eyes, and he got up a new creature. Rikki was disturbed, fearing that her husband had lost his mind. When she gave me her side of the story, she let her eyes roll back to indicate that she felt her husband had lost touch with reality. Meanwhile, Hans bubbled over with his newfound joy in the Lord and used every opportunity to visit us for prayer and fellowship. During one of our moments of prayer together, I prayed for one of my brothers in Holland who was gravely ill and gave no indication of knowing Jesus. Hans shared my burden for Edward.

When the end of their contract with the Catholic Mission approached, Hans and Rikki returned to Holland, and Hans went for a job interview. A Dutch charter company accepted him as a commercial pilot. Before they left, however, they spent their last day in Irian Jaya in our home. As Hans, Rikki, Janine and I were sitting together in our living room, I asked Rikki about her relationship with the Lord. She had, by now, given up her critical attitude and had moved toward a position of accepting the fact that her husband had become a Christian. But she said clearly that she was not one herself.

"Are you willing to ask the Lord to come into your life?" I asked.

"No, I'm not ready for that," was the answer.

I quoted the words of the father of the demon-possessed boy who had said: "I do believe; help me overcome my unbelief!" (Mark 9:24).

"Would you like to pray, and ask the Lord to make you ready?"

She nodded, so we prayed that the Lord would prepare her heart.

The next day the couple left, but they did not move out of our lives. Rikki kept up a regular correspondence with letters that sounded very positive, using spiritual-sounding expressions, but never stating clearly that she had accepted the Lord. Hans wrote and asked if I would like for him to visit my brother, the one for whom we had prayed. I agreed, of course. He made a social call, bringing greetings from us in Irian Jaya, and when he left he handed them a written account of his conversion.

The next day, Hans received a phone call from my nephew, Edward's son, Erik, who said he wanted to see Hans. Hans thought that Erik would come and ask him what business he had bothering his father with religious propaganda, but this was not the case. Erik had had his share of misery in life. He was into drugs, and he was ready to give up on life. He had read Hans' testimony and felt that maybe there would be hope for him also. Hans didn't have to talk long to lead Erik to Jesus. We were jubilant!

More than a year later, we left for the last furlough prior to our return to the States for retirement. As soon as it was feasible, we flew to Belgium to visit Janine's aging mother. Hans contacted us, asking us to come to Holland to baptize him, together with Rikki and Erik. In the car with Hans and Rikki, I said to her: "You wrote me very positive sounding letters, but you never told me what happened after the evening in our home when we prayed together."

"You mean you never got the letter in which I told you that I had accepted the Lord?" she asked. Evidently, that crucial piece of evidence had been mislaid by the Indonesian postal service.

"My conversion was not as dramatic as Hans'," she said. "After we left you, I became more and more aware of the fact that Jesus loved me and wanted me. I realized that He had heard your prayer and that I wanted Him also."

The baptismal service took place on January 3, 1993, in the Cross Road Church, an international fellowship of believers in Amsterdam. That was surely one of the highlights of my missionary career. I choked up as I baptized Hans, whom I call Onesimus, since I fathered him under such unusual circumstances. Only God could take a young pagan from the Netherlands, send him to Irian Jaya, and bring him back as a believer in Jesus Christ and a dear brother. He does work in mysterious ways!

One day, I stopped my motorbike in front of the house of the MAF pilot. He called me in and handed me several packages by way of "special delivery." Two envelopes contained order forms filled out by typewriter, obviously the work of a missionary colleague. The other package was wrapped in banana leaves, bearing all the marks of a Stone-Age culture. The contents turned out to be several wads of heavily soiled rupiah bills (Indonesian currency).

Although teaching in the Bible school was the main part of our job description, it was certainly not our only task. Most of the missionary work of the Alliance was done by missionaries who lived in the interior mountains of the island on isolated stations with radio transmitters and infrequent flights by MAF airplanes as the only link with the outside world. Our location in Nabire, at the shore of the Pacific Ocean, with access to a harbor and a more versatile airport, put us in a position where we would naturally be the middlemen.

Nabire boasted a thriving economy, mostly run by Chinese merchants who are unrivaled worldwide in their ability to carry out large enterprises with little overhead. Nabire had at least half a dozen Chinese stores with merchants who bent over backward to let the customer feel he was king. So the missionaries living in the mountains would send me orders or give their orders via the two-way radio. I would take them to a Chinese merchant who kept individual accounts for each of his customers, then send the groceries, building materials and other desired items to the MAF base for shipment to the outlying stations. I tried to keep my share of the administration down, but there were invariably glitches that consumed precious time.

All finances were channeled via the local Export-Import Bank of Indonesia, an institution that had studiously scrapped the word "efficient" from its dictionary. Depositing money or cashing checks would take hours of waiting and of being sent from one counter to another. Mistakes in bank statements were frequent, and the clerks were seldom ready to admit that they were the ones that were at fault. So the polite way of correcting discrepancies would be for me to write out checks to set things straight. After a few years of frustration, I lost my ability to evoke images of drive-in banks with ATM services and smiling, efficient clerks behind counters.

Not only were missionaries in need of provisions to keep going on their isolated posts, but the brethren of the indigenous church also needed help for their fast-developing districts which needed building material for new churches, kerosene for their lamps, diesel fuel for their generators and rice for their Christmas celebrations. I decided to set up various bank accounts for the different districts, and one of the local pastors, Thomas Degei, was trained to receive the money to be deposited into those accounts.

Most of the money that came in as crumpled-up wads of bills had to be straightened out and bundled together in denominations before the bank would even consider counting it. Dear Thomas would spend hours getting things ready, pedaling his old bicycle from the bank to the stores and back. This took at least part of the load off of my shoulders, but not all of it. The national brethren wanted to be sure that I cosigned every check and kept my finger on the whole operation. They seemed to believe that integrity and skin color went together.

Then there was the responsibility for our Lay Training Institute. Our fine-feathered friends never got tired of laying eggs. They probably knew what would happen to them if they opted for retirement. But those eggs had to be sold, sometimes hundreds of them a day. Usually this operation went smoothly, especially after we were able to buy a secondhand pickup truck. This saved us from having to perform precarious balancing acts while trying to transport five trays of eggs or more on the front of a motorbike. But sometimes the eggs would pile up, and we had to ask the Lord to help us sell them before the expiration date.

Once, we thought our prayers had been answered in a massive way when the owner of a local restaurant announced that he would buy all the eggs we had every day. The only condition was that he would pay us once a month. That's where the deal went wrong. We delivered faithfully, but on payday he came up with a long list of excuses. He was only able to pay a small part of his debt.

"Please, come back next week, and I'll pay the rest," we were assured. Next week, we had a repeat of the same. The debts piled up and the payments decreased accordingly. After several weeks of negotiations, I brought the matter to the students during one of the chapel periods and asked them to pray.

The next time I went to collect, I asked the man: "Are you a Christian?"

"No, I am Muslim," he hissed through the space left by two missing front teeth.

"The Christian students in our school are praying for you," I told him. This apparently put the fear of the Lord in him, and he paid his debt in full! After this we took him off the list of clients.

The heaviest burden was the local police office. Foreigners in Irian Jaya were not allowed to travel without a travel pass, issued and signed by the local police commander. Most of the time the sergeant in charge gave us service-with-a-smile, but often there was more smile than service. A special form was required to issue

JACK OF ALL TRADES

the required permission. This form was usually out of stock. I offered to copy the form on my computer; my offer was accepted in an underhanded way; that is, they were happy for me to print out the forms and fill them out as professional-looking documents, but they didn't want other people to know that they were not the ones producing the documents. So we made a secret pact: I would print and they would sign.

The form had to contain all the information regarding the person traveling, plus a recent passport picture in duplicate—one to be glued on the form and one for the police file. I never found out what the police did with the drawers full of duplicate passport pictures. For every little trip, whether it was a fifty-mile flight to Enarotali or 400 miles to Jayapura, those forms, stamped and signed, were an absolute must. Only when one traveled to Jakarta was this kind of permit not needed. Once I handed my travel pass to a police sergeant in Jakarta who wanted to know what it was and why I needed it. I told him, I didn't know. He said that these kinds of restrictions on travel had been lifted years ago in all of Indonesia. Somehow that word had not reached the outposts of the archipelago!

Very rarely was I able to obtain the required signature on my prefabricated travel passes without delay. Most of the time, I was told to come back the next day—or the day after. The Lord's grace was sufficient for this red tape, but I am convinced that nowhere is the tape redder than in Indonesia.

There were other more spiritual and less frustrating jobs to be done on the side which required a considerable amount of time and energy. I did not pastor a church, but I was regularly invited to fill a pulpit in one of the almost one dozen churches in the greater Nabire area. One Sunday, I attended a church and found out that I was announced to be the speaker at that service. Very rarely was I given a formal invitation to come and preach. The pastors of the churches would draw up preaching schedules for several months at a time and put my name on them without even consulting me. Some months, I preached every single Sunday, and since I taught a full schedule in the Bible school during the week, there were no days off. But I enjoyed preaching; consequently, I tried to keep abreast of the demands by always trying to be prepared.

For several years, the annual conference added to my job description the post of "Coordinator of Bible Teaching," which put me in an advisory position to all the high school-level Bible schools in the areas for which the Alliance assumed responsibility throughout Irian Jaya. I made an effort to visit each of the three or four schools once a year, and I was usually invited to their graduation exercises. During my administration, I brought together all the national personnel involved in Bible teaching to a seminar on the conference grounds at Pyramid. Missionaries from other parts of Indonesia who were involved in such ministries were also invited to come and have input.

We endeavored to raise Bible training to the highest level possible, but we were aware of the danger of overeducating young people to the point that they taught over the heads of their students. The Alliance has had a certain amount of success in raising the intellectual level of education. There are at least two individuals who grew up in a village situation, just evolving from the Stone Age, who were sent overseas, came back with a doctor's degree attached to their name and ministered effectively. But there were also those whose higher education did not serve them well and who were unwilling to go back to isolated places of ministry. The whole matter of higher education was a complex issue.

18

As Close to the End of the World as One Can Get

The tiny single-engine Cessna 206 took a sharp turn to the left as the pilot skillfully lined the plane up with markers on the small landing strip. This MAF pilot had it down to a science; he knew the landmarks exactly. He knew what his altitude had to be at a certain rock that projected above the rest and at which point his wheels had to touch down on the airstrip. To our untrained eyes it seemed as if the aircraft would touch the trees it was skimming, but over the years we had gotten used to such optical illusions.

So, after a flight of about twenty-five minutes we landed safely in Kegata. Bringing the plane to a full stop was not a problem, for although the strip was rather short, it had a slope of almost fifteen degrees, and the pilot had to give full power to make it to the top of the hill where he could turn his machine around.

Kegata is as close to the end of the world as one can get. I always had the impression that, if I would climb to the top of the mountain just north of the village, I would be able to see where the world ended. Kegata was countless miles into nowhere, separated from the rest of the world by thousands of square miles of jungle. Yet, people were living in this forsaken place.

The gospel had reached here almost thirty years before we touched down. Two single women, Marion Doble and Mary McIlrath, had tried to reach Kegata in the early fifties, but were forced to turn back because the trail was too hazardous. Harold and Mary (McIlrath) Catto, however, who had been appointed to Gakokebo, later trekked into the area. And a few years later, a male missionary walked in and built a shelter where missionaries could spend a few days on periodic visits. He also began the construction of the airstrip on which we had just landed.

Because of attrition of our missionary staff, visits to Kegata had become more and more infrequent. Although the small building that was to accommodate us for the three days of our visit was still standing, it was in serious disrepair. The first thing we saw, as we opened the door was a sign of habitation.

"Yuck!" cried Janine, who spotted three snake skins hanging over the rafters of the room above the bed. A search of the house did not reveal any snakes. Evidently, the reptiles used the facilities as their dressing room and only came to change their skins. Our presence would surely shoo them away, we hoped. I disposed of the skins, but to our horror fresh skins were back the next morning. Whether we wanted to or not, we would have to settle for the fact that we were sharing our hut with some of the Lord's other creatures. The small pythons of the area are not dangerous, but a snake is a snake, and the Lord did put enmity especially between snakes and women!

Even less than the presence of reptiles did we appreciate the sanitary facilities or lack thereof. The cabin had no indoor plumbing. Rainwater was gathered from the tin roof into a fifty-five-gallon drum. The toilet was outside, with a muddy trail of about ten yards separating it from the house. I suppose the original structure had been solid enough, but time had taken its toll. The floor of the outhouse needed emergency repair which we were unable to give on such short notice. So our visits to those facilities were accompanied by urgent prayer that the Lord would keep us from serious mishap.

Then there were medical needs that had accumulated between visits of missionaries. Yaws had never been eradicated from this valley, and we spent several hours giving shots of penicillin and handing out pills for dysentery and other serious ailments.

The main purpose of our visit, however, was to meet with the pastors of the area for prayer and encouragement. About one dozen of them showed up. We spent two days with them in a short-term seminar.

Leaving Kegata was almost as difficult as arriving. We opened our radio transmitter at the first ray of daylight and tried to call the MAF base in Nabire.

"What's the weather like in Kegata?" asked the crackling static-obscured voice.

The question wasn't easy to answer. High mountains surround the valley, and looking up to the sky is like looking up the walls of a cylinder.

"Clouds overhead, but some blue sky," was all I could answer.

"Sorry, its raining here, and the plane will not be able to take off for at least one hour."

The Kegata airstrip has a wind curfew, which means that landing the airplane after 10 a.m. was not allowed. We fervently prayed that the Lord would clear the sky in Nabire in time for the plane to take off and pick us up here. We had only one day of extra food supplies. If the flight was canceled for one day or more, we would have to live off the land, i.e., asking the people to help us with sweet potatoes. But the Lord heard our prayers, and when, by mid-morning, the airplane raced down the steep slope off the short airstrip and lifted its nose in the air, our hearts—and our bodies—soared with it.

One of my most memorable visits to Kegata occurred several years later. The indigenous church had organized a conference for all the pastors of the Kapauku churches west of the Wissel Lakes. For some of these men, this meant a trek of five days or more. The Kegata district had prepared for this conference by erecting a brand-new church building that could accommodate the more than 300 delegates. Most pastors came with two elders of their church. Many of the representatives showed up in Western clothing, but some arrived in their native penis gourd, carrying their bows and arrows.

Accommodations were rather primitive. The dining room was a large, extended building in the style of a native hut, with makeshift benches and tables which could serve only half of the crowd at a time. Meals had to be taken in shifts. The sleeping quarters consisted of another large hut-type building with a bark roof and a series of fireplaces in the middle of the floor around which the men slept at night. I took refuge in the mission quarters that showed even more signs of old age than at our first visit, but which was, in my opinion, still a better option than sleeping around the fire on a hard mud floor without a blanket. The nights were cold at this altitude of almost 5,000 feet, but as soon as the sun came up, the temperature soared to a comfortable 80°F or more.

The upbeat mood of the congregation, their joyful chants and deep love generated a warmth that was not influenced by any climatological factors. I had rarely attended such protracted meetings, some of which would last until late at night by the dim light of kerosene pressure lamps where the delegates showed no sign of weariness or desire to get things over with. There was no time consciousness here.

The committee that had organized the conference had invited me to bring the morning devotions and an evening message. I sat in on several of the business meetings, although I had no input in the discussions and could not vote. I learned that the conference wanted to send out four evangelists and their wives to an area several days travel west of Kegata called the

Jamor or Mushroom Lakes. This would mean traveling through a large swamp area infested by crocodiles. Unless canoes were available, this would be a very dangerous undertaking. I could not see how a family with young children could make such a trip. So I volunteered to contact the Mission and ask for financial support so that the MAF helicopter could be chartered. This, of course, was greeted with enthusiasm.

During the last evening meeting of the conference, the four young couples were introduced to the congregation. After the elders had laid hands on them to dedicate them to the Lord, there was a lengthy discussion about how to support the new missionaries. One of the delegates suggested that each pastor put a table in his church and announce that every member could donate items of clothing, household articles or any other useful objects.

Another one rose to his feet and, in a booming voice, said, "That is all fine, but we need to start right here and now. Let's set an example and put a table up front here where we can put our contributions." This was accepted by acclamation.

A large table was dragged to the front of the building, and the man who had brought in the motion was the first to wade through the crowd. Taking off his sweater, he put it on the table. I was deeply moved by the sight, because I knew that this man was not able to go back to his sleeping quarters and get another sweater. This was obviously all he had, and he actually needed it for himself.

His gesture opened the floodgates. People started streaming forward to put on the table not the extra things they had and could live comfortably without, but their very livelihood. While this scene unfolded, chants broke out over the audience. The Kapauku, like most of the Papuan tribespeople, are great improvisers. Soon the whole building was filled with a joyful noise, glorifying the Lord and thanking Him for the opportunity to be able to give sacrificially.

Sitting on the platform with tears in my eyes, I tried to picture what such a scene would do to people at home. Even the offerings that were taken up in the days of A.B. Simpson when people put their jewelry in the offering plate did not equal this demonstration of cheerful, hilarious and sacrificial giving. These poorest of the poor on this earth put the whole Church of Jesus Christ in the Western hemisphere to shame.

I was thrilled to see that a large percentage of those who came and laid their all on the altar were my former students. They had obviously learned more than I ever taught them.

I have always had an aversion to statistics and evaluations. Throughout the years, I have resisted evaluating my colleagues or myself, which, for a long time, was a point of contention between the Irian Jaya field leader and me. I could never reconcile the modern urge to evaluate with Paul's exclamation: "Who are you to judge someone else's servant? To his own master he stands or falls. And he will stand, for the Lord is able to make him stand" (Romans 14:4). I even resisted the temptation to evaluate myself, based again on Paul's words to the Corinthians: "I care very little if I am judged by you or by any human court; indeed, I do not even judge myself" (I Corinthians 4:3). I do not believe either, of course, that one should merely float on life's ocean without any sense of purpose or direction, but if our eyes are fixed on the Lord, our evaluations belong to Him.

As a young Christian, I had, due to a lack of consistent fellowship with the Lord, struggled with emotional instability. A brother in Christ counseled me and said: "What you need is to have your quiet time. Why don't you get up half an hour earlier every morning, read your Bible and pray?" I decided to follow this advice and set my alarm clock to half an hour earlier than my usual rising time. To my chagrin, I promptly slept through the alarm. I tried it again the next day, and the same thing happened. After several weeks of struggle, I decided to pray and ask the Lord why I couldn't get out of bed to have my daily devotions. I didn't hear a voice from heaven, but I clearly knew that God said: "If you really want to get up half an hour earlier in the morning, why don't you go to bed half an hour earlier the night before?" I decided to follow this advice. From that time on, getting out of bed was never a problem.

On the mission field, I kept up the habit. It became even more urgent when people started coming to our door at the crack of dawn. If I hadn't read my Bible and prayed before 6 o'clock, I found that I never got around to it. Once the daily routine was established, the early morning hour became the highlight of the day. My Bible, a notebook and a cup of coffee led me to intensive study which furnished me with a wealth of material that not only thoroughly nourished my soul, but also gave me an abundance of substance for sermon notes and Bible lessons.

In Nabire, I had made a small office in the annex to our house which served as a storage place and quarters for our house help. There was a combined bedroom-living room space and a bathroom on the other side of the wall of my study. The father of the family living there was a student in the Bible school, and his wife, Elesina, helped Janine in the kitchen and with house cleaning and laundry. Every morning, about half an hour into my quiet time, I could hear Elesina get up and start the day by calling upon the Lord. The tribespeople do not believe in silent prayer. When I say that Elesina called upon the Lord, I mean that literally. This faithful woman never missed a day. Her routine became a special blessing to me. I thought of the influence this sweet hour of prayer would have upon her children. Every morning, when they opened their eyes, their first sight would be their mother on her knees praying. I am sure this must have left a lasting mark upon their young lives.

After my own quiet time, I would go back in the house and take a cup of coffee to Janine who had by then finished her own devotions. We would drink coffee together in bed, celebrate the beginning of a new day and pray together. This habit has become hard to break. We haven't even tried.

I consider that the time spent with the Lord in the morning, the reading of His Word and the writing of notes, is the only thing of real importance I ever did on the mission field. Everything else evolved from that moment in the day.

Jesus words sound so simple: "Only one thing is needed. Mary has chosen what is better, and it will not be taken away from her" (Luke 10:42). The Lord wanted me to be at my post, and He did the rest. Maybe little Jonathan was right, who, after finding out I was a missionary, said, "Oh, you're like my daddy; you do nothing."

19

. . . Such Sweet Sorrow

The time had come for us to retire. "When our father and mother leave us to go back to their home country, we are giving them a feast." The students who were sitting in front of me in my study looked at me very seriously and somewhat defiantly. Behind those words was a rather sharp confrontation which these students of the eastern part of the island were having with the fellows from the western part who had challenged and opposed their plans.

The tribespeople expect departing friends to give "souvenirs" to the ones left behind. The missionaries, who, of course, are everybody's friend, are taken to be a rich source of such tokens of friendship, especially when they are about to go home to retire. We had been concerned that we would have to give away all our earthly possessions to our intimate friends, the number of which was increasing daily. We had prayed and asked for prayer, since we would never have been able to satisfy everyone even if we stripped ourselves to the point that we would leave with only the clothes we wore.

Several people had come around, suggesting that we prepare ourselves for our departure by giving them something by which they would remember us (preferably something expensive), and that we throw a lavish farewell party. The answer to our prayers came from a very unexpected source: the students of our theological school whom we thought would be the most demanding. They themselves would prepare the feast.

The students from the east must have done a very good job in convincing the Kapauku tribe. Not only did none of our students come around to ask for farewell presents, but also we were sent off in a spirit of genuine love and gratitude, a spirit that was prevalent in all of our good-byes.

It all began and ended in one of the local churches in Nabire. About nine months before our departure date, I was invited to speak at a series of revival meetings. The choir greeted us with a newly composed chant: "They came to bring us the gospel, and now they are leaving. They came for the last time." It was moving, although not exactly true; we would visit that church several more times. But, obviously, our dear friends were preparing themselves for the time we would not be with them anymore. Then came the invitation from the Kebo Bible School which we had known from its inception in 1963, the place where we had served for about thirteen years. Would the *Tuan* (Indonesian for Mr. or Sir) come and hold spiritual emphasis meetings for the students?

There was no longer a mission presence in Kebo, and we wondered where we would stay on this occasion. When we landed early in the morning, the entire student population, almost 100 men strong, awaited us at the airfield, and we were welcomed with a newly composed song. In the tribal language, they sang that we had come before to preach the gospel to them and that now we came for the last time to say good-bye. Tears flowed.

The Rev. Naftali Pigome, the director of the school, now lived in the house we built, our former home. Consequently, we were taken to the house that had belonged to the Walter Posts, the first Alliance missionaries to Irian Jaya. The house was in perfect condition. It had been cleaned for our arrival and, although we had brought our own food, we received a steady flow of guests who brought us vegetables, eggs and fish. Even people whom we had known before to be confirmed materialists did not want to receive any payment for the things they brought. A few days later, we left amidst hugs and tears and flew over Paniai Lake to go to Enarotali where another farewell service had been planned.

Just prior to our departure date in Nabire, the district superintendent organized a combined farewell service for us in which the twelve Alliance churches of the area participated. One of our former students preached. After that, a representative of each church stepped forward and presented us with a gift. The Dani tribespeople came with a quarter of a pig that was given to us with the necessary ceremony. But the Kapauku wanted more. In the afternoon, several hundred of them assembled in another church at the edge of town and held a service in their own language. I gave my testimony and told the congregation how the Lord had called Janine and me into His service and how He had directed us to Irian Jaya.

After the sermon, we were treated to a performance in which a man and a woman played the role of the young John and Janine who had come to the Wissel Lakes thirty-seven years before. We saw ourselves accompanied from the airfield in Obano, to the little boat with outboard motor that ferried us over to Enarotali. There, they dramatized how we had steeped ourselves in language study of the tribal tongue and how, after a few months, we were moved to our first mission station, Gakokebo, at Lake Tigi. The woman then played Janine's role as nurse, asking the people who were standing around, "Do you have a stomach ache?" "Do you have diarrhea?" then she would hand out pills.

Then one of the preachers stood up and commented on the scenes by telling what had become of the boys and girls I had taught at the Dutch elementary school. Some had become important government officials. What touched me deeply was the way they put our ministry in perspective. Scenes were repeated when we moved to Enarotali to teach at the Kapauku Bible School, and later when the school moved to Kebo, and finally when we moved to Nabire. "Janine" in the form of the lady who represented her, was busy, in the meantime, diagnosing the symptoms of the sick people, and "John" kept on teaching while the commentator kept everything in perspective by recalling the fruit that our ministry had produced. If we had summarized our own ministry in this way, it would have been terribly presumptuous, but to hear it from the mouth of others was a deeply moving experience.

The service ended with the appearance of a Kapauku woman who was completely dressed in black and decked out with all kinds of items that represented the old heathen Kapauku culture. She came to Janine, who was told to take off the ornaments one after another—the head covering, the beads, the shells and the net bags. Those were then given to her as presents. After this, she was handed a white robe which she put on the woman. In conclusion, Janine put a Bible in her hand, the New Testament in the Kapauku language. The commentary was: "This is what you did for us!"

What else could we do, but praise the Lord?

They loaded us with presents of net bags beautifully adorned with yellow orchid fiber. One young man gave me a pouch with a long string of cowry shells which, I found out later, were part of a bride price received at the wedding of his sister.

Just before our departure, I spoke at the graduation exercises at the Walter Post Theological School. Janine and I hugged each of the students, and the tears flowed freely. It was a deeply emotional experience to say good-bye to the ones we had taught and learned to love. Rev. Sumilat saw us off at the Nabire airport. In a most uncharacteristic way, he hugged both Janine and me. There were tears in his eyes. We had known that taking leave of Irian Jaya would be difficult, but we did not know it would be that emotional. At the same time, it was a precious memory which we would not have wanted to miss.

Thus ended a major chapter in our lives. We had arrived in Irian Jaya for the first time as newlyweds on January 12, 1958. We left the place that our four children call "home" for the last time on May 31, 1995.

Appendix

Final Report to the Irian Jaya Field Forum

by John and Janine Schultz

Psalm 48:14: "For this God is our God for ever and ever; he will be our guide even to the end."

For those of you who want to know in detail what we did during this last conference year, please read our previous year's report. We did basically the things we have been doing for years, and we have enjoyed doing them.

Therefore, we would like to give this, our last report, a wider scope and take a bird's-eye view of what happened in our lives since we arrived on the field of Dutch New Guinea in January 1958. We were probably the most uneducated and most unprepared missionary couple the Alliance ever sent out. Neither the Alliance, nor we ourselves, were aware of this, and our unawareness was probably a great blessing.

Both of us had only a three-year Bible school training at an institute in Brussels which prepared young people for ministries in Belgium. All which was then our loss, we now consider gain because of Christ, since we came to the field without any prejudice apart from the opinion that Europeans were better than Americans, that Dutch were better than Belgians, with one exception (John's opinion), and that Belgians were better than Dutch, with one exception (Janine's stand).

Our missionary career started in Enarotali, where we were immersed in Kapauku language study. . . . After about eight months of this regime, our first daughter, Ruthy, was born; she was followed by an almost yearly succession of babies. We tried to squeeze four children into our first term, but did not quite make it. Our younger daughter, Viviane, was born shortly after the beginning of our second term.

Three years and three babies after our arrival, Janine was told that she had to pass her final language exam if we wanted to return for a second term. She not only did her finals without much trouble, but she also picked up English on the side, as well as Indonesian.

We spent half of our first term in Gakokebo as teachers in the Dutch language V.V.S. (Continuation School—grades four through six which was subsidized by the Dutch government). All this was dumped on us without much ceremony or introduction, and we learned to swim.

When we came back for our second term, the Kapauku Bible School had been moved to Kebo and had been changed into an Indonesian language school in order to accommodate all the tribes with which the Alliance was working at that time. We spent a couple of good years together with the Walter Posts, and after the Posts had to leave because of serious health problems—and never returned to Kebo—we floated to the top, and John became the head of the Kebo Bible School. We spent thirteen wonderful years in Kebo, and our kids, who still consider Kebo their home, retain precious memories of this period.

John's desire had always been to teach. He tried to pursue this urge after high school, but when the Lord called him to the mission field, it seemed that a teaching career had to be put on the altar. But the Lord, who had given the desire, fulfilled it in His own time and in a better way than we could have dreamed.

We were in Kebo when the "Act of Free Choice" was about to take place, and the area around the Wissel Lakes was in turmoil because of it. We had to evacuate twice in order to evade getting caught between the warring factions. At one point we thought our ministry had come to an end. But the Lord broke through in a wonderful way. We remember a prayer meeting during our conference in Pyramid in 1969 when we had the clear conviction that the enemy had been defeated. When we returned to Kebo, the war ended within a few days.

One of the deepest trials in our family was the sickness of Michel in 1974. His emotional problems became so acute that he had to be taken to Sydney, Australia, to be hospitalized. For several years this remained one of the most incomprehensible episodes in our lives. It was not until several years later that we realized how the Lord used this for His glory, and we were able to thank Him for it. At the time we were going through this testing, we felt it would have been easier to lose a child through death than to witness this mental and emotional breakdown.

Michel's sickness brought us to the States for an extended furlough. We spent two-and-a-half years in Atlanta on a six-month visitor's visa which miraculously kept on being renewed until a new visa for Indonesia was granted and we could return to the field, leaving Ruthy and John Paul behind in the States.

At the request of the Nabire district we moved to Nabire to start the Walter Post Theological School. The National Church gave the name "Walter Post" to the school. Initially, Walter himself objected to the honor, but the Lord overruled by taking him up to glory. To him that would love life and see good days, my advice is not to refuse if the church wants to honor you by dedicating one of its institutions in your name!

We had the honor, the challenge and the joy of starting the school from scratch. There was no ground, no money to build, no personnel to teach, no curriculum and no lessons. The Lord provided step by step for each of those needs in an exhilarating way. When we look at the campus and the students who graduated over the last seventeen years, we say: "The LORD has done this, and it is marvelous in our eyes" (Psalm 118:23).

We leave you all with heavy hearts. We believe the Lord clearly called us to work in this country. We also believe He clearly calls us to leave it at this time. We know that what we have accomplished here does not amount to anything great on a universal scale, but we trust that it has a place in the coming of the kingdom and the return of the King.

God bless you all!

> Respectfully submitted,
> John and Janine Schultz

Family Update

All our children were born in Enarotali. After finishing their education at the M.K. school in Sentani and at Dalat School in Malaysia, they enrolled at Toccoa Falls College (TFC) in Toccoa Falls, Georgia.

There, *Ruth,* our oldest daughter, met Tim Hall, an M.K. from Cambodia. At the time of this writing, Tim is the pastor of the Alliance church in Marianna, Florida. Tim and Ruth have three children: Joshua, Sarah and Jason.

John Paul (JP) graduated from TFC and married Judy Harvey, an M.K. from Guinea, Africa, also a graduate of TFC. They have served as house parents in Irian Jaya and at Dalat School and have now been reassigned to Ivory Coast Academy. They have three daughters: Alexis, Stephanie (twins) and Jordana.

Mitch (Michel André) graduated from TFC with a degree in Missions. He met his wife, Elaine Blekking, at the college, and they married in 1983. After serving in two pastorates, they were appointed to Great Britain as church planters.

In June of 1998, Mitch almost lost Elaine due to a brain tumor. After surgery, she went through a long period of rehabilitation to regain her faculties of speech, reading and writing. In August 1999, the Lord called home their twelve-year-old son, Travis, who suffered from an inoperable brain tumor. They have two other children: Breanna and Brett.

Viviane attended TFC and graduated from the University of Missouri with a degree in elementary education. In 1984, she married Matt Miner, who grew up in Malaysia, where his parents were on the staff of Dalat School. In 1995, they were appointed as house parents at Dalat School. They have three children: Melanie, Maria and Max.